D1493261

THE ENGLISH COTTAGE

THE BRITISH HERITAGE SERIES

Uniform with this Volume

THE ENGLISH COUNTRY
HOUSE
By RALPH DUTTON

THE ENGLISH GARDEN
By RALPH DUTTON

THE ENGLISH CASTLE
By HUGH BRAUN

THE ENGLISH ABBEY
By F. H. CROSSLEY

ENGLISH CHURCH CRAFTS-
MANSHIP
By F. H. CROSSLEY

THE GREATER ENGLISH
CHURCH
By HARRY BATSFORD and
CHARLES FRY

THE CATHEDRALS OF
ENGLAND
By HARRY BATSFORD and
CHARLES FRY

THE PARISH CHURCHES
OF ENGLAND
By J. CHARLES COX and
C. BRADLEY FORD

THE OLD TOWNS OF
ENGLAND
By CLIVE ROUSE

ENGLISH VILLAGES AND
HAMLETS
By HUMPHREY PAKINGTON

THE OLD INNS OF ENGLAND
By A. E. RICHARDSON

THE COUNTRYMAN'S
ENGLAND
By DOROTHY HARTLEY

THE HEART OF SCOTLAND
By GEORGE BLAKE

THE FACE OF SCOTLAND
By HARRY BATSFORD and
CHARLES FRY

THE LAND OF WALES
By EILUNED and PETER LEWIS

THE SPIRIT OF IRELAND
By LYNN DOYLE

OLD ENGLISH CUSTOMS
AND CEREMONIES
By F. J. DRAKE-CARNELL

THE OLD PUBLIC SCHOOLS
OF ENGLAND
By JOHN RODGERS

OLD ENGLISH HOUSEHOLD
LIFE
By GERTRUDE JEKYLL and
SYDNEY R. JONES

* ENGLISH VILLAGE HOMES
By SYDNEY R. JONES

* THE SEAS AND SHORES
OF ENGLAND
By EDMUND VALE

* THE HEART OF ENGLAND
By IVOR BROWN

* THE SPIRIT OF LONDON
By PAUL COHEN-PORTHEIM

* Out of print for the duration of the war.

Published by
B. T. BATSFORD LTD.
15 North Audley Street, London, W. 1
and Malvern Wells, Worcestershire

I THE VETERAN

*From an Eighteenth-Century Painting
by an unknown Artist, in the Dyce
Collection, Victoria and Albert Museum*

THE
ENGLISH COTTAGE

By

HARRY BATSFORD

Hon. A.R.I.B.A.

and

CHARLES FRY

Illustrated from Photographs,
Diagrams and Drawings

SECOND EDITION,
REVISED

LONDON
B. T. BATSFORD LTD.
15 NORTH AUDLEY STREET, W. 1, and
MALVERN WELLS, WORCESTERSHIRE

2813

First Published - - *October* 1938
Second Edition - - - - 1944

MADE AND PRINTED IN GREAT BRITAIN
FOR THE PUBLISHERS, B. T. BATSFORD LTD., LONDON
BY THE DARIEN PRESS, EDINBURGH

PREFACE

Two reasons to justify a book on the English Cottage might be :

(*One*) that its study, or at least the perusal of its illustrations, would tend to stimulate the public to a more united effort to defend the rather precarious existence of these little buildings, which, often beautiful in themselves, are nearly always a vital ingredient in the beauty of their patch of landscape ; and

(*Two*) that a study of their craftsmanship and technique, which represent the common denominators of English taste and construction through many centuries, would help to bring about the wider appreciation of a tradition that often expresses itself as completely in the cottage as in more ambitious buildings—a tradition of which, despite improved amenities, all members of the community might still avail themselves with benefit : the builder and manufacturer equally with the architect and craftsman, to say nothing of that vast lethargic public whose demand creates their wares.

Even at the present time, only a comparatively small minority respects the value and beauty of the old cottages, both intrinsically and in relation to their surroundings ; and it seems urgently desirable, in such restless and ruthless days, that their cause should enlist a wider range of sympathy, backed with publicity and money, if those that remain are not to share the fate of so much else that was beautiful in this country, and has been relegated, with contempt and indifference, to that busy bird of prey, the demolition contractor.

Cottages are common-sense buildings ; their study requires little technical knowledge and demands little technical jargon. Its range can be indicated in a few simple questions : What is a cottage ; of what is it built ; how was it built ; for whom was it built ; how was it occupied ; how was it improved and enlarged ? An attempt has been made in these pages to answer each of these questions by a clear statement. For practical purposes it has been found necessary to treat the different structural methods employed in separate chapters, each devoted to the technique derived from a material. A preliminary glance is given to the peasant's cote of the Middle Ages, in which was evolved the laborious cruck construction—the ancestor of half-timber —that survives in occasional examples in western, central and northerly districts. The post-and-truss technique that superseded it and became the national vernacular (which to-day we call half-timber) is dealt with in two chapters, one concerned with its construction and the other with its local types. Cottages of mud, or cob as it is now generally called, were built side by side with the others from early times, and their construction is described in the chapter that follows. Then comes stone, the use of which, except in specially favoured districts such as the Cotswolds, was rare until the eighteenth century, classified according to its regional appearances.

Roofing, a complex and confusing subject in its range of local variation, is next surveyed under its three main headings of Thatch, Stone-slates and Tiles, and is followed by a section on the weather-proofing of walls, often necessitated by later disintegration, which provided the pleasant expedients of Tilehanging, Weatherboarding, Brick-nogging and the like. A chapter on the cottage interior, its arrangement, fittings and furniture, is followed by some remarks on cottage life and folk through the centuries. A final chapter deals with the decay of the old fabrics during the last century and their frequent replacement by brick, the cult of the model village, the recent fashion for reconditioning cottages, and speculations as to the future of that part of Cottage England that remains intact.

The development of accommodation—planning seems a too formal word to use in this connection—is a subject to which we have only been able to refer incidentally throughout these chapters. It is closely identified with the changing course of rural life, from the communal husbandry of the open fields to the " private profit " farming of the present day, and the evolution of the rural worker from villeinage to his present none too enviable state. But this latter subject, so vast and difficult of generalisation, it has been thought better to attack, with what success the reader must judge, in an opening chapter. A volume on cottage accommodation and the life lived in it has been projected.

Thus the general scheme of the book. But the authors are under small illusion as to its value were it not backed by a wide pictorial documentation, in which the work of many photographers finds a place, and which, it is hoped, provides a better bird's-eye view of the whole subject than has appeared before. In addition, they have been privileged to include a number of line drawings, details and plans from the more specialised works of such authorities as Mr. S. O. Addy, Mr. W. Curtis Green, R.A., the late Sir Guy Dawber, R.A., Mr. Basil Oliver and Mr. Sydney R. Jones ; others are from the work of Mr. Edwin H. Gunn and Mr. A. H. Powell, or have been specially prepared by Miss Norah Davenport. Without the valuable body of otherwise unavailable information assembled by Mr. C. F. Innocent in his *Development of English Building Construction* the book would have been impossible in its present form, and the authors would like to take this opportunity of expressing their debt to this book, and to the books of other scholars, which have been resorted to so frequently during the preparation of the text.

Finally, it may be added that the Cottage is here understood to mean the home of the rural labourer, craftsman and smallholder (excluding the yeoman and farmer, whose dwellings form a subject in themselves) during the period from the later Middle Ages to the nineteenth century.

H. B.
C. F.

September 1938

ACKNOWLEDGMENT

The Publishers must acknowledge their obligation to the following photographers whose work appears in the illustrations, namely, Mr. Harold H. Camburn for figs. 95, 98; Mr. W. A. Chislett for figs. 69, 83; the late Brian C. Clayton for figs. 12, 14, 25, 88, 89, 90, 107; Mr. A. Colebrooke for figs. 74, 85, 101, 114, 134; Mr. Fred H. Crossley, F.S.A., for fig. 18; Mr. Stephen Cubitt, for fig. 64; the late W. G. Davie for figs. 21, 28, 38, 39, 40, 41, 118, 119, 120; Mr. J. Dixon Scott, F.R.P.S., for figs. 5, 6, 7, 9, 10, 23, 35, 36, 42, 45, 47, 48, 56, 63, 67, 78, 79, 82, 99, 100, 113, 116, 123, 137, 138, 148, 149; Eagle Photos, Cheltenham, for figs. 22, 29, 30, 75; Mr. Herbert Felton, F.R.P.S., for figs. 24, 31, 32, 33, 43, 58, 59, 60, 71, 72, 96, 106, 108, 124, 125, 127, 135, 143, 150; Fox Photos for figs. 44, 52, 104, 115; Mr. Leonard Gayton for figs. 11, 46, 66; Messrs. Gibson & Sons, Penzance, for fig. 53; Mr. F. A. Girling for figs. 3, 84, 103, 105; Captain C. G. M. Hatfield for figs. 62, 70, 73; Humphrey and Vera Joel for figs. 4, 34, 76, 86, 112, 121, 122, 144, 145; Mr. Kevis, Petworth, for fig. 117; Messrs. Dorien Leigh for fig. 129; Miss Sylvia Lewes for figs. 50, 54, 55, 68, 77; Magazine Photo Service for fig. 81; Mr. R. R. Rawkins for figs. 51, 87; Mr. T. E. Routh for figs. 13, 61; Mr. John H. Stone for figs. 2, 16, 26, 49, 57, 102, 128, 136; Mr. Will F. Taylor for figs. 8, 27, 37, 65, 80, 93, 94, 97, 109, 110, 111, 126, 141, 142; and Mr. Gordon Turnill for figs. 15, 91, 92. Fig. 17 is reproduced from *The Development of English Building Construction*, by C. F. Innocent, by kind permission of the publishers, The Cambridge University Press; the drawings on *pp.* 17 and 21 are from *The Evolution of the English House*, by S. O. Addy, by kind permission of Messrs. George Allen & Unwin; and the frontispiece and fig. 133 are from originals in the Victoria and Albert Museum.

CONTENTS

2　THE GOSSIPS: Broadway, Worcestershire

3 SUFFOLK PASTORAL: Withermarsh Green

THE ENGLISH COTTAGE

I

COTTAGE ENGLAND

Six centuries have worked their steady changes on the English landscape. The tangles of marsh and fen have been drained, and tidied into arable and pasture ; the forests which covered vast tracts have shrunk to a sprinkling of wood and copse ; and of the heaths, little now remains but an occasional patch of " common," slashed by roads and fringed by cottages or suburban houses. Around the villages, with their nondescript modern accretions, the open fields of our forefathers have long since been replaced by a chequer-work of enclosed farmlands, while the " wastes " that were their perquisite have dwindled or vanished, and much of the dense woodland timber has been sacrificed as fuel, or for the building of forgotten ships. Some small part of this remains, however, in the fabric of our cottages, in tough old beams which even now can show the marks of the wright's axe, recalling a time when the English house was almost literally hewed out of the English forest, and when English oak supplied the framework for a smaller architecture which can still to-day, in its surviving examples, convince us that it possessed the three requisites of Sir Henry Wootton's famous axiom : " commodity, firmness, and delight."

Collectively, these cottages have witnessed much of the laborious process by which the land has been disciplined into its present productivity, while the responsibilities of its upkeep have been gradually shifted from the community to the individual ; and have shared in the development and decay of that once vital cell of our national life : the village. As they arose to replace the tumbledown hovels of feudalism in decline, so in their turn, and in the mellow beauty of their age, they are being superseded by the bungalows and " building schemes " of an era of mass-production. That they provide a lesson for all time in the seemly and unpretentious use of materials to their best advantage is patently obvious. Yet apparently it is a lesson difficult of application to-day ; for as one fine example after another is allowed to perish in the gradual disintegration of our countryside, neither skill nor taste (which are never altogether absent) seem able to contrive a tolerable substitute for this vernacular of a simpler age. Here the word " architecture " would seem a definite misnomer, for it is unthinkable that these little houses were ever conceived by their builders in such ambitious terms. Utilitarian in purpose, the beauty they achieved has a spontaneous, almost fortuitous quality that would seem to result from the instinctive handling of native materials by craftsmen who, in Innocent's well-chosen words,* " were in a stage of culture in which technical ability produces works of art naturally and unconsciously, unlike the technically skilled workers of present-day civilisation, who can only design ' works of art ' after much training."

It has become almost a commonplace to comment on the quiet fitness of these old cottages to their surroundings and to the purpose they were built to serve. That they should have become such part and parcel of the landscape is not surprising, for their materials are largely those of the countryside to which they belong, and their development has constantly expressed its social changes. Their maturity is reflected in the weathering of their fabrics : the silvery toughness of old oak, the tinted and lichened peace of Cotswold stone, the deep rosy glow of Kentish tiles. The great oak forests provided an almost inexhaustible supply of timber for a technique of framing which achieved, perhaps, its richest effects, and remained most constantly in evidence, in the Western Midlands and along the Welsh Border. Later, substitutes were often found for the original wattle-and-daub filling of the walls, such as the brick-nogging of Hertfordshire and Hampshire, the plasterwork of East Anglia, the tilehanging of Surrey and the weatherboarding of Kent, which still lend character and colour to their neighbourhoods. While cottages built of mud, or cob as it is now generally called, without the support of a timber framework, have always existed, and are still common in the South-west, it was only towards the eighteenth century that the more general wood-and-wattle began gradually to be replaced, in some districts by brick and in the North by the widespread stone construction that we know to-day. This, appropriate as it is to its surroundings, cannot, however, bear comparison with the little world of architecture created from the limestone of the Cotswold grazings, an architecture that arose in the wool villages and townlets of the wold proper, and spread on either hand throughout the diagonal band of the material that stretches

* C. F. Innocent : *The Development of English Building Construction.*

4 THE COTTAGE GATE, WROXTON, OXFORDSHIRE

5   HALF-TIMBER AT CROPTHORNE, WORCESTERSHIRE

from Dorset to Lincoln, reaching its perfection in the early years of the seventeenth century and leaving as a legacy some of the most perfect cottage groups that this country can show.

Generally speaking, the golden age of cottage building was between 1550 and 1660, though our present study ranges from the Middle Ages to the Industrial Revolution and beyond. It is a study so interwoven with the life of the countryside and the evolution of our domestic building that in a short book it is only possible to deal with it in the strictest terms, and define the cottage as a house built for the occupation of a rural labourer or craftsman during the period under review—rejecting such modern twists of meaning as " the residence at a pleasure resort " helpfully supplied by one dictionary. For the major part of this period it is important to remember that, though country life was in a state of almost ceaseless flux, the English remained predominantly a rural population, whose crafts and industries were for the most part distributed over the countryside. At its beginning, agriculture was still carried on almost wholly upon traditional co-operative lines, with the village farm as the unit of life and work. At its close, the open fields and pastures in which all had once enjoyed their rights and holdings, even the wastes which, by time-honoured usage, had provided " fern or heather for litter and thatching, hurdle-wood, and tree-loppings for winter browsing, furze and turves for fuel, acorns and mast for swine, as well as large timber for fencing implements or building," * had submitted to the chequerwork of hedge and wall, and husbandry had passed irrevocably from the province of the community to that of the individual.

This was effected by a gradual process of transition between two periods of revolutionary change : one caused by the drift from the manor at the close of the Middle Ages, and the consequent disintegration of feudal methods of life and work, which we call the Agrarian Revolution ; the other resulting in the transfer of most of the common lands to individual ownership during the reign of George III, and the almost universal adoption of the " private profit " system in agriculture which we know to-day. The best age of cottage building thus lay between two worlds : an old world of toil on a land in which all enjoyed some sense of proprietorship, lightened by traditional festivities and games, and infused with a deep-seated sense of obedience to established authority

* Lord Ernle : *The Land and its People.*

in matters spiritual and temporal; and a new world of enterprise and adventure in matters of trade, industry, politics and the humanities. For village England it marked an important and constructive phase with which our old cottages now provide in many ways the most tangible link. Therein lies their sociological significance. Their artistic significance is more obvious, in that they represent one of those periodical florescences of native craftsmanship made possible by a change in economic circumstances : a spontaneous culmination of centuries of work on familiar materials by familiar methods, as important in its less spectacular way as the outburst of poetry which almost simultaneously transfigured our national drama.

At the dawn of this age (*c.* 1550), in spite of the encroach-ments of sheep-farming, by far the major part of the land was still cultivated on the open-field system, and by far the major proportion of rural workers still retained some stake in its soil, if only in the form of rights of pasture and common. Tudor resourcefulness had done much to counteract the results of two centuries of agricultural depression and unrest, but the Agrarian Revolution had worked its havoc on the country-side, breaking immemorial ties of land tenure and service, releasing a flood of vagrancy and reducing many a thriving village to little more than a few rotting hovels around the church. Recovery was effected to a great extent by the consolidation of a new class of yeomen and tenant farmers, whose well-being had become a particular concern of Tudor policy. While the landlord tended to segregate himself from rural life in a new mansion in a park, the responsibilities of rural organisation were shifted more and more on to their broad shoulders. These men were often employers of labour on no inconsiderable scale, a labour that was increasingly easy to find, for the inducements of service at a wage, as opposed to the bare livelihood to be extracted from a few strips of soil grown sterile through centuries of over-cropping, had, as the feudal grip relaxed, caused an increasing drain on the village farms. Nevertheless, there can have been few families at this time who had altogether relinquished their private rights of husbandry, and it may be supposed that, while some of the younger members might prefer employment as hired labourers or estate servants, the father and his first-born would still likely enough make a scanty living by the old laborious methods, cultivating their scanty crops, pasturing their thin beasts, collecting brushwood, and cutting turf on the commons. Though the village remained a self-contained community, individual specialisation was also coming to the fore in the trades and crafts, such as those of the smith, the weaver, the miller and the tanner, to say nothing of the carpenter, the thatcher, the tiler, the dauber, the mason, and those other rural craftsmen responsible for the fabric of the English cottage. New industries were likewise being developed, and a wide range of them, from smelting down to knitting, was being established from village to village over the countryside.

A radical change had, in fact, come over the village. By the close of the sixteenth century, though the corporate spirit was still to a great extent maintained in the working of the open fields, Tudor local government had vested much of the authority of the manor in a group of officers elected by the parish community, under a landed magistracy responsible to the Crown. A much wider field of enterprise was already open to the individual, who, as unemployment grew rarer, could often make his choice between the old round of communal agriculture as practised by generations of his forbears, and farm work at a wage. Here, if the returns were meagre by modern standards, the patriarchal life of the farmhouse, which generally provided lodging for all its dependants, was by no means irksome, and the fare of its kitchen probably abundant and varied. With the seventeenth century, the Mop Fair, which was to endure in many places far into the nineteenth, thus became a familiar feature of the local market-place. At this rough-and-ready equivalent of the modern labour exchange, the men would assemble in groups, each decorated with the emblem of his calling : the carter with whipcord in hat or buttonhole, the shepherd tufted with wool, the hedger with his bill and the fieldworker with his shovel. As new industries were developed, many villages became little hives of energy in one of them or another. There were, for instance, the nail-making carried on until quite recent times in the cottages of the Birmingham district, the chair-turning of the Chilterns, the lace-making of Devon and Somerset, and the Gloucestershire knitting, to name only a few among many. Looms whirred and clacked throughout East Anglia and the West Country to supply the thriving export trade in textiles, and the graziers and staplers of such a district as the Cotswolds had for some time enjoyed the benefits of boom conditions, evident in the small-scale stateliness of their local architecture. Here and elsewhere where trade flourished or craftsmen congregated, as in the weaving district around Lavenham and

Kersey in Suffolk, an unusual sense of costliness often seems
to pervade the little houses, that is expressed in the carving
of a barge-board or corner-post, the enrichment of a gable or
chimney, perhaps occasionally in the addition of an oriel. In
the quieter agricultural regions, besides the timbered farmhouses which were arising, each the centre of its own mesh
of fields, stout new cottages were replacing the decayed,
chimneyless cabins of the medieval village—many of which
latter were to linger on, nevertheless, far into the seventeenth
century. The village was coming into its own as a small

A PLUNDERING SCENE, VALUABLE AS A CONTEMPORARY
REPRESENTATION OF A TUDOR VILLAGE

From Holinshed's Chronicle (1585).

epitome of the national life and work, and its new beams and
bright plaster seemed to symbolise the awakening consciousness
of the inhabitants to the improvement of their lot.

It was a very real improvement, despite the many small
pinpricks of local authority, despite the bland tyranny or
indifference of the squire and the parson, and the frequent
squabblings and intolerances that, then as now, were liable
to poison village life. There is evidence that, already, the
farmer was often abusing his privileges as a man of substance,
particularly in the use of the commons ; nevertheless, as the
Hammonds have well put it,* " whatever the pressure outside
and whatever the bickerings within, it remains true that the

* J. L. and Barbara Hammond : *The Village Labourer*.

6 WEAVERS' COTTAGES, KERSEY, SUFFOLK

7   A LAKELAND COTTAGE, BORROWDALE, CUMBERLAND

common-field system formed a world in which the villagers lived their own lives and cultivated the soil on a basis of independence." In these respects the country was ahead of its neighbours, and the old cottages stand as emblems of that sense of "rugged individualism" which had its roots in the village, and was to become the keynote of national development, both here and in the New World, in after years.

The construction of cottages from the Middle Ages to the death of tradition in the nineteenth century, their craftsmanship, and the variations in material and technique in different parts of the country, are the main subjects of this study. But it is a study that is largely sterile unless some indication is provided of the social conditions which brought these little dwellings into existence, and the kind of men for whom they were built. These, to summarise the last few pages, generally belonged to one of four classes :—

The smallholders, who either owned land freehold by "squatters' rights" which they had originally cleared from the forests, or else maintained their hereditary holdings on the village farms.

The part-time labourers, who probably maintained rights of pasture and common which enabled them to keep a beast or two in addition to their farm employment at a wage, and provided them with small timber and fuel.

The specialised craftsmen, such as the weaver, the smith, the tanner, the carpenter and so forth, who probably retained at least similar rights.

As the period drew to its close, a sprinkling of tradesmen, who might also be smallholders or commoners.

These men, and the thrifty multifarious life they represented, were directly responsible for the metamorphosis that had transformed the countryside from a primeval to a pastoral landscape. They had hacked away the forests and drained the swamps, and established by their toil a system of agriculture which, rudimentary and unimaginative as it was in many ways, supplied the national larder through the good times and bad of our history. The organisation of their life and work formed the germ of a democratic system ; their crafts and trades were the seed of a vast industrial harvest. It is to them, rather than to the more resounding names, that we owe what is most virile and enduring in our national life ; and it seems sad that it should have been they, rather than the others, who were sacrificed for our evolution into a mercantile and manufacturing nation.

The village entered on the eighteenth century without perceptible change in its major institutions. Though more land was gradually being enclosed by the estates and farms, there were still, at an estimate, some 160,000 small freeholders, while the number of the entirely landless remained a very modest proportion of the rural population. Agriculture was practised on much the same methods as had obtained in the Middle Ages, but the growing exhaustion of the soil was causing anxiety to the more thoughtful, and, as the century progressed, certain writers were propounding scientific theories which were being put to a successful test by the more progressive of the landowners and farmers. Jethro Tull with his drill; Lord Townshend, who reintroduced the practice of marling on light lands, and made other important experiments in the rotation of crops; Coke of Holkham, who carried these experiments to a triumphant conclusion on his great Norfolk estate, were drawing curious eyes upon them from all parts of the country. But the new scientific farming was impracticable except upon enclosed lands; and the new scientific farming was becoming a very urgent necessity if the land was to be preserved for agriculture at all. Enclosure thus became the order of the day, and few would have questioned its advisability if it had been carried out in a spirit of fairness to the smallholder and commoner, and, as Arthur Young suggested, sufficient land had been reserved for each cottage at least to support a cow. But vested interests were at work; and the landed proprietor and farmer were determined that, if enclosure was to be effected at all, it should be effected preponderantly to their advantage. The myriad private bills which, in two remarkable spasms of energy between 1770 and 1780, and between 1800 and 1820, were rushed through Parliament, arbitrarily sealed the fates of smallholding communities all over the country, and deprived them in a swift succession of blows of most of their rights in a soil for whose cultivation they had always been responsible. There was no appeal save by a Bill in Chancery. The open fields, the pastures, and, by a still less tenable injustice, the commons themselves, were absorbed into the already swollen territories of the estates and farms, and, by the accession of Queen Victoria, save for such insignificant " greens " and " commons " as we know to-day, mostly of a poor soil that has always resisted reclamation, England was ensnared in its

8   AT LECKHAMPSTEAD, BUCKINGHAMSHIRE

9   A TIDY HAMPSHIRE THATCH GIVES CHARACTER TO THIS NEW FOREST COTTAGE

10   AT BILTON, WARWICKSHIRE

11 SELWORTHY, SOMERSET: a Study in the Picturesque

mesh of hedgerow and wall, while the rural population had resolved itself into its three present categories of landlord, tenant farmer and hired labourer.

The effects of the Industrial Revolution, by which industry was reorganised and concentrated in the towns, were equally drastic in country districts. Lord Ernle, in his important and delightful book, *The Land and its People*, well summarised the changes that took place. "Everywhere," he wrote, "manufacture and agriculture were simultaneously reorganised on those commercial lines which facilitated increased production at reduced cost. Farming ceased to be a subsistence and became a trade. The united effect of the two reorganisations was to sweep away many small freeholders, tenant farmers and commoners who had lived by the cultivation or use of land in combination with the practice of domestic handicrafts. Their places were taken by the large corn-growing, meat-producing farms which met the needs and fashion of the day. The organisation of the village, in which wealth and poverty, employer and employed, were almost imperceptibly graded into one another, was broken up. With the destruction of the primitive framework went the traditions of the peasant, his inherited ideals, his ancestral customs, his habitual solutions of the problems of existence."

The country, in fact, under the stress of war and industrial expansion, had become little more than "a factory of bread and meat for the towns." While the Napoleonic Wars lasted, the prolonged demands they made on the national economy largely concealed the effects of these changes. It was left for the era of peace to bring about a disillusion as bitter as that we have experienced in a later age. To quote Lord Ernle once again: "The years 1814-36 were the blackest period in the history of the agricultural worker. The depth of misery into which he then fell is the measure of the advance that he has subsequently made. Distress was universal. The war was over; but 'Peace and Plenty' proved a ghastly mockery. Large tracts of arable land fell out of cultivation, considerable areas were even untenanted. Less and less labour was required. Wages fell to pre-war levels; but even at the lowered rates, work was hard to find and harder still to keep. . . . The effect of the rural changes was now brought home with tremendous force. The sale of their labour on the land had become the workers' only means of livelihood. The domestic handicrafts which supplemented their earnings had been swept into manufacturing centres. . . . All that they

c

had formerly produced for themselves, they now had to buy. They felt the full pressure of prices, and the lower their wages, the keener the pinch."

The tradition of sound building, which had for so long expressed the cottager's individualism and pride of proprietorship in the soil, lapsed during those hard years, never to be recovered. In the poverty and disillusion that ensued, the old cottages were often allowed to fall into terrible dilapidation, and, save on a few estates where a " model village " might serve a landowner's vanity, were replaced, if necessary, by featureless brick boxes, coloured a bilious yellow or a livid pink, that shared a mushroom growth with the Council School, Workhouse and Methodist Chapel of the Victorian village. It is unnecessary to follow the vicissitudes of the rural worker further ; with the Victorian period he largely ceases to be a householder in the old sense but becomes a tenant, and one who likely enough finds difficulty in persuading his landlord to keep his walls in repair and his roof weathertight. Even to-day, with the increasing importance of his rôle, he remains perhaps the hardest worker at the lowest pay in our industrial system. To the townsman he is apt to appear either sentimentally picturesque or mildly ridiculous ; while his qualities of perseverance and quiet assurance, maintained through a whole later period of neglect and want, are largely overlooked. As a recent writer has well put it : * " His is the oldest of man's occupations and the most necessary ; nor without him would there have been anything that is. Townsfolk speak or think of him as slow and stupid ; but he is the most highly skilled labourer of all men. Even though the machine is more and more performing his larger tasks, he still uses, with an incomparable deftness of hand and eye, tools that in a thousand years have become almost human limbs. The most accomplished mechanic of the factories could not plash and weave a hawthorn hedge with a billhook without maiming the green life and his own person : but the countryman who does that daily would not take five years' apprenticeship to set the tools of a turret lathe to the thousandth of an inch."

Such qualities are well expressed in the fabrics of our old cottages, which, moreover, for the closer student of the countryside, reflect certain stubborn characteristics which have always distinguished one English district from another, one county from the next, within the national mould. Nothing,

* F. J. Harvey Darton : *English Fabric.*

for instance, could be more contrary than the timbered cottage of the Western Midlands, with its tiled roof and bright infilling of plaster, and that of Dorset, small, stony and reserved beneath its deep-sunk thatch ; yet both, with many another local type, owe their existence to the same tradition built up through generations of ordered life and work on the land, and their decay to its destruction in the commercial intoxication of the last century. Such simple fabrics can often afford a more direct insight into the national character than mansions and public buildings, and, moreover, they are redolent of those curiously blended qualities of equability and individualism which have always constituted the most distinctive ingredients of the English ethos. The decline of their tradition represents the decline of elements which we can ill afford to obliterate from our national life.

The helpless sense of flux, which to-day pervades most conditions, tends, perhaps, to draw us nearer than we have been for many years to the fragment which remains to us of Cottage England, standing up bravely beside the shoddy indecency around, and suggesting a comfort more real than drains or mains could supply. Until the balance of the national economy has shifted more in favour of the countryman, and the village has resumed some of its old multifarious activities, it does not seem likely that its tradition can be revived or reborn. Nevertheless, those who care for the dignity of their surroundings can, in the meantime, and with the aid of the bodies specially formed for the purpose, do their share in preserving such vestiges of the ancient beauties as remain : the many tracts of country still unspoilt, with their quiet population of cottages, so congruous with the landscape and the life of its soil.

II

THE PEASANT'S COTE

The development of the cottage, in most of its earlier phases, follows closely on that of timber construction in this country. The former abundance of the material in almost every district, coupled with the rudimentary nature of transport and communications, recommended its use, even when there was a natural supply of stone, for the majority of buildings. Throughout the Middle Ages, churches and fortifications remained the most consistent exceptions to this tendency. At the same time, there is small evidence to show that, even before the Conquest, much resort was ever made to the almost universal " blockwork " construction of the European coniferous belt—a construction which, incidentally, was to find its way to America with the early settlers, and is still employed in the backwoods of the United States and Canada as it is among the mountains and forests of Central Europe and Scandinavia. By English timber building we mean the construction of houses on a timber *framework*, by a process of evolution ranging from a rudimentary method common throughout the later Middle Ages and enduring in remoter districts well on into the seventeenth century (which was based, as we shall see later, on a simple structural misconception), to the developed form, still hardly superseded, which was to produce the complex and picturesque " half-timber " of Tudor and later times. Here it may be remembered that sometimes the actual fabric of this framing is of a far greater antiquity than the building it now supports. As in time the supply of home-grown timber began to diminish, it became customary to adapt the woodwork of older houses for use in new ones—a process, incidentally, of real advantage where the material was oak, which grows harder and tougher with age and usage. Thus, the timbers of our cottages (together, of course, with much of the fabric of our churches) may often supply the tangible links between the village of to-day and its ancestor of five or six centuries back.

In appearance, the village of the Middle Ages would have differed strikingly from its comfortable, if somewhat amorphous, descendant of the present day. It was an altogether smaller and flimsier affair, a rough cluster or straggling street of fragile little dwellings, probably whitewashed and rudely thatched, each having its small curtilage, or " toft," for the growing of

12

12 A GABLE-END AT DIDBROOK, GLOUCESTERSHIRE, showing the complex constructional development from an ancient cruck framework

13 SUTTON BONINGTON, NOTTINGHAMSHIRE   14 DYMOCK, GLOUCESTERSHIRE

EXAMPLES OF CRUCK CONSTRUCTION

the home produce, enclosed perhaps, like that of Chaucer's poor widow, by a stake fence. The chief landmark, as to-day, was the church, its new stonework, crisply finished with white plaster, contrasting with the decayed and poverty-stricken appearance of some proportion at least of the cottages. At its largest, such a village can seldom have housed more than a few hundred souls, whose poultry and beasts made free of the thresholds and fouled the muddy ways between the houses. The almost unique employment of the menfolk was a rudimentary and painstaking husbandry, performed under the authority of the manor by which they were held in villeinage, a toil that began and ended each weekday with the light, and was alleviated by an occasional rough festivity and the simple ritual of the church services. Most of a man's waking hours were spent on the bare, strip-patterned fields of the communal farm adjoining the village, ploughing with the ox-team, sowing, digging and so forth, or on the meadow pastures and heathy " waste." Seen from a bird's-eye view, the settlement would have appeared frugal and struggling in the extreme to modern eyes—a rather pathetic little clearing in a loneliness spreading away vast and shaggy on every side.

It is here that the story of the English cottage begins. During the earlier Middle Ages it is probable that the peasant's house was seldom more than a rough shanty, built from the ground either of wattle-and-daub or mud, and roofed with a thatching of straw or reed, or even with turves of growing grass or moss. So fragile were these little houses that they were liable to be shaken down by any violent storm ; indeed, a thirteenth-century thief would debate the relative advantages of forcing a door or simply breaking down a wall. A villein behindhand with his dues might well be punished by the pulling down of his house over his head—a form of retribution not unknown to Scottish and Irish landlords even in the last century. The almost tent-like facility with which a house could be demolished or set up dates back to very ancient times, and is instanced in the Irish saga of *The Feast of Bricru* quoted by Professor Macalister, in which houses erected for guests were broken into by a crowd of terrified women, and one was nearly pushed over, causing much heart-burning till it was straightened by a powerful thrust. It was a general cause of complaint in the Middle Ages that villeins absconding from their manors would knock down their houses and carry off the materials to be erected elsewhere.

As the period advanced, probably towards the close of the

D

fourteenth century, a new type of construction came gradually into use, which, always cumbrous and quite obsolete to us to-day, represents unquestionably the first stage in the development of a national style of timber framework building, and is still traceable in the older cottages and farm buildings of many parts of the country. Our knowledge of it we owe in the main to the work of two scholars, Mr. S. O. Addy and Mr. C. F. Innocent, and it would be ungracious to pretend that the brief account of its methods that follows would be possible without a frequent resort to their researches.* This mode of construction is generally called " cruck-building," though " fork-building " and " curved-tree construction " are also used to describe it. Roughly, its method was the setting up of wooden forks, or crucks, generally shaped in a slight curve, each pair of timbers forming the split halves of the same tree-trunk. These timbers met at apexes of equal height, and supported a horizontal ridge-pole which carried the rafters, the crucks themselves being strengthened by lateral tie-beams. Such a construction, in its simplest form, would provide the framework for a house, rectangular on plan, somewhat of the shape of an inverted boat, the roof descending in one sweep from the ridge-pole to the ground; but it is doubtful whether houses of this sort were ever common, or, if so, survived for long. Only in one building in this country, the Walt Disney-ish little structure known as Teapot Hall at Scrivelsby in Lincolnshire (15), has it come down to us, and that must be regarded to some extent as a freak.

It is believed that cruck-building had its origin in a simple type of hut, built on forks and a ridge-pole, which was used in remote times as a temporary, and sometimes portable, shelter by herdsmen at their summer grazings. But when the form came to be applied to more permanent buildings, the disadvantage of cramped quarters beneath inward-curving walls must soon have become apparent, and a method had to be devised for retaining the heavy crucks still considered essential for supporting the weight of the roof, at the same time providing vertical walls which would afford a greater internal accommodation. The fallacy underlying the whole cruck principle was, of course, that the ridge-pole bore the weight of the roof, and thus required substantial support from beneath—a fallacy which it is strange nowadays to realise persisted in many country places until well into the seventeenth

---

* S. O. Addy: *The Evolution of the English House*. C. F. Innocent: *The Development of English Building Construction*.

15 TEAPOT HALL, NEAR SCRIVELSBY, LINCOLNSHIRE

16 THE SIMPLEST TYPE OF ONE-STOREY COTTAGE: Mickleton,
Gloucestershire

17 THE CRUCK FRAMEWORK OF A DEMOLISHED HOUSE
AT MIDHOPE, SOUTH YORKSHIRE

18 COTTAGE OUTBUILDING AT STEVENTON, BERKSHIRE

century, and was only completely discredited with the general adoption of the " post-and-truss " construction for timber-framed buildings.

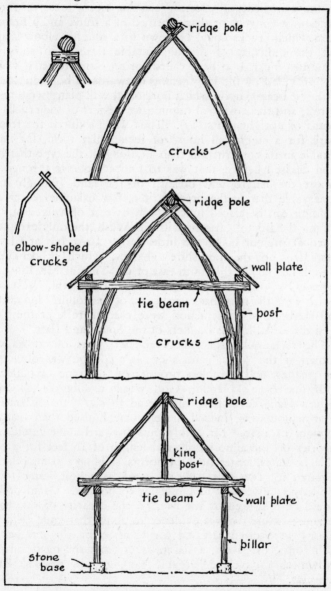

ridge pole

crucks

elbow-shaped crucks

ridge pole

wall plate

tie beam

post

crucks

ridge pole

king post

tie beam

wall plate

pillar

stone base

CRUCK, AND EARLY KING-POST, CONSTRUCTION

The problem of the vertical wall was first solved, it has been suggested by Mr. H. Hughes and Mr. H. L. North from their examination of a number of old cottages in Snowdonia,* by the expedient of selecting angular tree-trunks, or single pieces of a convenient shape formed of a trunk and a branch, from which crucks could be hewn to a roughly elbow-shape. But the difficulty of finding suitable timbers in sufficient quantities must soon have called for an easier remedy, which was provided by the lengthening outwards in both directions of the tie-beams, upon which horizontal wall-plates were made to rest, and their external framing to the feet of the crucks by means of upright posts (17). Thus was produced the framework for a single-cell house of rectangular form, far more durable in its construction than anything of the type that had been devised before, that was to find acceptance throughout almost the length and breadth of the land—though it is remarkable that, at the present time, few examples of cruck-building can be traced much south or east of a line roughly joining the Bristol Channel with the Wash, the only exception noted at present being the little Barley Mow Inn at Clifton Hampden on the Berkshire Thames, which is definitely, though not far, to the south-east of it. This, as Mr. Innocent remarks, is probably due to the fact that " the West and North were the most backward parts of the country in culture, and methods of construction were used there after they had been discarded by the builders of the South and East."

The rectangular space between two pairs of crucks was known as the " bay," and a one-bay cottage was obviously the smallest and humblest product of this type of building. " Of one baye's breadth, God wot! a silly cote," wrote Bishop Hall, developing his theme to show that Chaucer's poor widow was, indeed, little worse housed than many a cottager of 1610. Mr. Addy puts forward some interesting theories on the almost universal length of 16 feet for a bay. This, he states, represented the normal stabling accommodation required for two pairs of oxen, and, as a unit, came to be applied as universally to houses as to bothies. Grain or hay would be measured by the bay, *i.e.* the capacity of one bay's storage ; while there is evidence to show that later medieval houses were often assessed for taxation by the number of their forks, or gables, as is apparent from the medieval due known as " gavelage " (gable tax), or, in monks' latin, *forcagium.*

* *Old Cottages of Snowdonia,* by H. Hughes and H. L. North.

As will be seen, a one-bay cottage can have offered only the most meagre accommodation for a labourer and his family. The obvious method of enlarging it would be to build on longitudinally by further bays, and this was carried out in many cases, one long building often housing several families, rather in the manner of a modern slum row. Mr. Addy has suggested that the number of bays permitted a householder was proportionate to his holding in the common fields, but, whether this was the case or no, many instances are traceable in which the single bay was enlarged, either by lean-to "outshuts," or by longitudinal extensions independent of

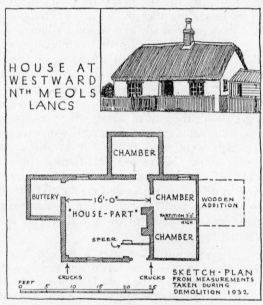

HOUSE AT WESTWARD NᵀᴴMEOLS LANCS

CHAMBER

BUTTERY ←— 16'-0" —→ CHAMBER WOODEN ADDITION

"HOUSE-PART" PARTITION 7'0" HIGH

SPEER CHAMBER

CRUCKS CRUCKS SKETCH·PLAN FROM MEASUREMENTS FEET TAKEN DURING 0 5 10 15 20 25 DEMOLITION 1932

From Addy's " Evolution of the English House."

the principal cruck framework. The demolished cottage at North Meols used by Mr. Addy as an illustration, and reproduced from his book by kind permission of its publishers, furnishes an excellent example of the extent to which a single-bay dwelling on crucks could be enlarged, and forms a case in point of the historic predilection of the English countryman for outbuilding, which can be observed in so many old cottages at the present day (18).

Early cottages usually consisted of two rooms, the hall, or "house-part," which contained the hearth and was the only

part of the building to be heated, and the bower, or " chamber,"
which provided sleeping accommodation, at first for the
women only. It soon became customary to add an outshut
pantry, or " buttery," for the household utensils and duties
on the opposite side of the house-part to the chamber, often
in the form of a lean-to, contrived by carrying down the slope
of the roof in a catslide to cover a small boarded enclosure,
framed on upright posts. Other chambers could be added in
the rear by the same method, as is shown on Mr. Addy's plan,
a curious feature of which is that the original chamber, divided
into two rooms by a later partition, did not here, as must have
been usual, form part of the cruck construction proper, but
was added by extending the roof over wattle-and-daub walls
to upright corner-posts at the end of the building.

Cottages of this type were, in their original form, seldom
of more than a single storey, with a floor of trodden clay and
a roof open to the rafters. There was no chimney : the fire
in the house-part, which was often shared with the animals,
was either laid on the floor itself or in a flat iron pan in the
centre of the room, the smoke being left to escape as best it
could through the door and the deep little windows (*wind-holes*,
wind-eyes), which were used rather for ventilation than for
lighting, and might be closed by framed blinds, called
" fenestralls," of cloth, canvas, or, from the Tudor Period,
linen soaked in oil. The variegated smells and smoky gloom
of these interiors is perhaps better left to the imagination ;
but it is richly reconstructed for us by Bishop Hall in the lines
already referred to :—

> Of one bay's breadth, God wot ! a silly cote,
> Whose thatched sparres are furr'd with sluttish soote
> A whole inch thick, shining like black-moor's brows,
> Through smok that down the head-les barrel blows :
> At his bed's-feete feeden his stalled teme ;
> His swine beneath, his pullen ore the beame :
> A starved tenement, such as I gesse
> Stands straggling in the wasts of Holdernesse ;
> Or such as shiver on a Peake-hill side,
> When March's lungs beate on their turfe-clad hide . . .

The timber framework of the houses was built by the
village carpenter, or wright, who, at first no more than a
servant of the lord of the manor, seems, by the twelfth century,
to have acquired a special standing in the village community,
often paying rent for his holding without service, and, as
time went on, receiving fees for his work on materials supplied

20 A SIXTEENTH-CENTURY COTE, FROM THE
GRIMANI BREVIARY

19 A WINTER SCENE OUTSIDE A
FIFTEENTH-CENTURY COTTAGE

21 WATTLE-AND-DAUB CONSTRUCTION AT WEST BURTON, SUSSEX

22 WATTLE HURDLING AT WARMISTER, GLOUCESTERSHIRE

by the lord. Later still he was to provide, and receive payment
for, both labour and materials, while by the fifteenth century
(the period *par excellence* of English medieval woodwork), an
industrious wright serving a large community might employ
his own paid staff of skilled craftsmen. It was he who
selected suitable oak in the forests for crucks and beams,
splitting the trees with beetle and wedge, and trimming and
squaring the timbers on the spot with the axe before trans-
porting them by ox-sledge to the site. Here the framework
of the building was largely jointed and fixed together on the
ground with heart-of-oak pegs, or, less frequently, with iron
nails ; and the whole village would likely join in the considerable and exciting task of " rearing " it into position with
ropes and chains, free drinks being afterwards served all
round, as is shown by substantial items in several old accounts.
Earlier cruck buildings were erected without foundations, the
timbers which rested on the ground being charred to prevent
rotting, but after a while it became usual to set the cruck-ends
on rough bases, or stylobates, of undressed stone, or, later,
the whole building on a low foundation wall.

The framework erected, the completion of the house was
largely left to the wallwright, or dauber, with the specialised
assistance of the thatcher and plasterer in their own spheres—
though in some country districts wattle-and-daub and thatching seem to have been undertaken by the same workmen, as
witnessed by the old title, " thatcher and dauber," which
still occasionally survives. In the great majority of houses
built on the cruck principle, the filling in of walls was effected
by the traditional method of weaving twigs or brushwood in
and out of upright sticks, or laths, inserted in the divisions
between the oak timbers to form a kind of hurdling, then
throwing on the daub in layers on either side, giving time to
dry between each application, the material generally being
composed of clay mixed with chopped straw or cow-dung,
trodden into the necessary softness and pliability of consistence.
It must be remembered that with most cruck buildings still
in existence the walling is a later substitution. As Mr. Innocent
has pointed out, many an old stone barn or cottage in the
North of England can reveal within a complete timber framework on crucks, that remains firm and unshaken when the
outer shell is dismantled (17), in confirmation of the fact,
already stated, that the use of stone for small and unpretentious
buildings, even in what we would now call a " stone district,"
was practically unknown until a later period. Though brick

was reintroduced into England during the Middle Ages, the material continued to be chiefly imported from the Low Countries for many years to come, and its use was therefore precluded, by price and scarcity, for all except the more elaborate buildings. Cottages built of mud (cob), without a timber framework, were, of course, common throughout the Middle Ages in many parts of the country, notably in the South-west, but the examination of these is reserved for a later chapter; nor must we forget the so-called " clunch " houses of East Anglia, built of a kind of hard chalk marl.

The structure completed, the walls were usually finished, inside and out, with a coating of lime plaster. A whitewash finish was preferred in most cases, but local variations of tint existed, as they do to-day, such as the ochre-yellow common in the North, the light green of Derbyshire, and the " noggin " houses of Kent, in which the outside walls were covered by a traditional patterning of white flowers against a background of red or black plaster. Mention must also be made of the " orchil " still to be found in remote parts of Yorkshire and the North, a somewhat unpleasant hue of deep " Reckitt's blue " extracted from liverwort, but probably used more for internal than external purposes.

The larger proportion of medieval cottages were undoubtedly roofed with thatch. We know little of the medieval thatcher, save that he seems to have enjoyed a reputation from his capacity for food and drink while engaged on his job, nor of his methods, owing to the temporary nature of his materials, which comprised a wide range, including straw, reeds, rushes, heather, ling and so forth, according to the resources of the neighbourhood. The varieties of thatching still to be seen about the country are discussed in more detail in a later chapter, and probably afford a fairly good insight into medieval methods. At the same time, other types of roofing were consistently in use for buildings of a smaller sort. There were the turves of grass or moss, already referred to, for cottages of the humblest kind, generally laid on beds of heather or ling, whose fresh green colouring must have contrasted pleasantly with the whitewashed walls. There were the timber shingles, or " slats," now practically obsolete in this country but still used with pleasant effect in the " colonial " building zones of the United States, which were usually bedded on turves, rushes or heather, and fastened to the rafters with oak pins, or, in one part of Yorkshire at least, with the smaller bones of sheep. There were the stone-slates common wherever there was a supply of suitably fissile stone, which are still one of the glories of our limestone building belt and are practically indestructible, though heavier roof timbers, set at a flatter pitch, are required to bear their weight. And there was at least some use of burnt-clay tiles.

Such, so far as can be traced, were the ingredients of the first fairly durable type of labourer's dwelling in this country. But before going on to deal with its further development, it may be well to consider briefly another type of house, that of the smallholder, which gained a footing in some parts of England where the feudal system was more loosely enforced,

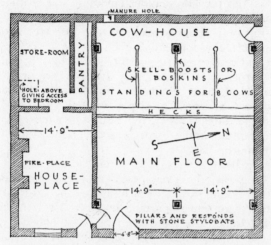

PLAN OF THE FORMER "COIT" AT RUSHY LEE,
UPPER MIDHOPE, WEST YORKSHIRE
From Addy's "Evolution of the English House."

such as the lonelier parts of the North. In this, the dwelling was combined under one roof with a barn, or "shippon," to form what is still called in Yorkshire a "coit," generally built as a dependency of a larger farm for occupation by one of its hinds. We are permitted to reproduce the plan of an example at Rushy Lee in West Yorkshire examined and described by Mr. Addy. Here the shippon, which forms the main part of the structure, is built in a form suggestive of the aisled basilica of classical times, being supported by two pairs of wooden pillars on stone stylobates, with responds in the north wall. Thus, the shippon itself is divided into two aisled bays, while the house forms a further bay to the south, outbuilt under the

E

same roof. The plan of the latter is suggestive of many later detached cottages in that the house-part to the east, which rises the whole height of the building, is flanked to the west by a store-room with a partitioned-off pantry, from which a ladder ascends to a chamber above. The shippon contains stalling for eight cows, with an outside cattle entrance, divided from the threshing-floor by a " heck " over which the animals could be fed. There are two other external doors to the building, one to the dwelling and a larger one to the threshing-floor ; but an internal door from the house-part gives direct access to the shippon, so that in bad weather the cattle could be fed without the householder emerging out-of-doors. The whole building is self-contained under one roof, the " aisle " walls rising only about a man's height from the ground, so that the external doors are framed in the eaves. It was a compact and convenient (if possibly somewhat uncomfortable) type of structure, that probably had its prototype in the arrangement of many old Norse homesteads. Sometimes it was built on the cruck principle without aisles (or perhaps with a single outshut aisle), but more often it seems to have conformed to the arrangement described, which was obviously the more appropriate.

In the earliest buildings of this " aisled basilica " type erected on posts, the ridge-pole was presumably supported by central " king-posts " reaching to the ground. This manifestly inconvenient arrangement could, however, be modified, it came to be discovered, by shortening the post and resting it on a cross-beam, which in its turn transferred the weight of the ridge-pole to the walls—an arrangement which is shown in its simplest form in the diagram on page 15. Elementary as its logic seems to-day, it registered an important stage in the transition of the post-and-truss construction described in the next chapter, an essential feature of which is that the tie-beam can rest upon the wall-plate, and not the wall-plate upon the tie-beam as in former cruck buildings (17), reversing the whole misconceived system of stress and strain upon which the latter were based. Whether or not this innovation was introduced from abroad, as some writers hold, or whether it was simply due to the horse-sense of a school of carpenters who, after all, had probably by this time much of the achievement of English church roofing to their credit, must remain a debatable point, though it is interesting to observe how closely the little post-and-truss cottages of Flemish fifteenth-century miniatures (such as those

23   A ROADSIDE COTTAGE, DUCKLINGTON, OXON

24 RUBBLE AND THATCH AT TADMARTON, OXFORDSHIRE.
Note the bake-oven, outbuilt and thatched, and the well beneath

of the Grimani Breviary), and of the backgrounds of such
paintings as those of Gérard David and, later, Pieter Brueghel,
conform to the methods of a later school of English carpentry.
Many of these small painted examples (19, 20, 132) can easily
be visualised set down in Hampshire to-day without appearing
at all incongruous or alien to that most English of landscapes.
Be it as it may (and the course of evolution, one must
remember, is apt to be controlled by more than one current
on such uncharted seas), this discovery brings us to the
threshold of perhaps the most important phase of our present
study, and it will be better to reserve its discussion for the
next chapter.

III

THE TIMBER-FRAMED COTTAGE

Tudor England, imagined in bird's-eye perspective, was a countryside in rapid transition. It was a shaggy England still, much overgrown with fen, marsh and forest, but the tangle was being beaten back around the agricultural clearings, and many acres of heath and waste were being caught up into the deer-parks of new mansions replacing the grim little fortresses of the feudal aristocracy. These palaces of a " new rich " could dispense with moats and fortifications, and were arising, vast and picturesque, among unenclosed parterres and formal gardens. The open fields of the communal farms remained, but they were shrinking, and everywhere more land was submitting to the chequerwork of hedge and wall that was forming around the timbered steadings of the yeomen and tenant farmers, and more green was showing among the arable, where the amassed holdings of emancipated villeinage were being laid down to pasture. The village was changing, too, by rapid stages. Among the hovels of the feudal peasantry, new cottages and village farms were arising, stoutly built to two storeys of oak beams and white plaster, roofed with tiles or thatch, and here and there touched, for the first time, with decorative craftsmanship. There was a briskness over the face of the land. The " merry England " of Tudor dreams was stirring and waking to life, and though much squalor and misery remained, the air was one of optimism. The Englishman was beginning to experience for the first time some degree of personal freedom, and the desire, and opportunity, of improving his lot.

It was as much from such tendencies as from a logical process of evolution that the later English cottage derived. One of its most outstanding features is its individualism, that obstinate variety of plan, outline and texture that makes its classification the despair of writers who would regiment it into watertight regional compartments. Pronounced local characteristics exist, it is true, and these are dealt with in detail in later chapters. But it is so often the exception which proves the rule. These little dwellings arose to house a nation of " rugged individualists," whose personal tastes and vanities are constantly displayed in the fabrics. They have generally suffered much adaptation throughout their long lifetimes, and can reflect the vicissitudes of the English rural worker at almost every stage. Built in response to a clear demand for better housing, they underwent a widespread decay during the stagnation of rural life that followed the Enclosure Acts of the reign of George III, from which in some cases they have never properly recovered; while right through the period embraced, there was always a tendency for farms or manor-houses to be subdivided into cottage tenements as they were abandoned with the shrinkage of the smaller gentry and yeomen, or discarded with the demand for more up-to-date accommodation, thus adding to the quota of village buildings another type of cottage group, of which the planning and detail reflect a decidedly more ambitious conception than the buildings properly under survey. The recent fashion by which old cottages are " discovered " and reconditioned as week-end retreats for town dwellers forms, incidentally, an amusing, or sometimes tragic, modern reversal of this older tendency.

A large number of more capacious yeomen's houses do, of course, remain to us from the later Middle Ages, and these are often classed as cottages in an easy way. But if by cottage we mean the home of the rural worker of post-feudal times, and of the smallholder as distinguished from the farmer, we find the most prolific period of building, at least on a post-and-truss framework, to fall roughly between the years 1550 and 1630, with a more intense sub-period of 1570 to 1620. In many districts Village England was very largely rebuilt during this short phase, a state of affairs which did not escape the watchful eye of the Tudor authorities, as is witnessed by a statute of 1589, which provided legislation " for avoiding of the great inconveniences which are found by experience to grow by the erectinge and buyldinge of great nombers and multitude of cotages which are daylie more and more increased in manye parts of this realme." This act laid down that no one was to build or convert existing buildings into cottages without setting apart at least four acres of land to each. Those exempted from the rule included seafaring folk, tradesmen and craftsmen, which perhaps helps to explain why the cottage of this period always flourished most in districts not exclusively given over to agriculture. It was also strictly enjoined that no cottage was to be occupied by more than one family.

Though timber-framed houses constructed on the post-and-truss method, or even, in out-of-the-way places, on crucks, continued to be built until the dawn of the eighteenth century, the use of brick had by then become much wider, or of stone where local resources allowed. Throughout most of the sixteenth and seventeenth centuries, however, timber-framing remained the vernacular mode of construction, at least for smaller buildings, so that it will be well, before going on to examine regional types, to recapitulate very briefly the structural method in use at this most prolific period of production.

The construction of a post-and-truss building varied little with the size of the house. Horizontal balks of timber, or cills, were laid on low foundation walls of brick or stone; into these, upright posts were inserted at intervals, mortised and tenoned, any additional securing being obtained by the use of oak pins. The posts were at first closely placed at intervals equal to their own width, a type of construction known as " post-and-pan " (31, 36). Later, as timber became more scarce and dear, the posts were placed at much wider intervals, so that in many instances the panels of the framing were approximately square (34). In more important buildings, these panels were often enriched with circles, cusps or quartering, generally formed of timbers cut out of the angles of crooked boughs, that would have been useless for ordinary structural purposes. This elaboration, as will be seen, was carried to far greater extremes along the Welsh Border than in the South or East, where for cottages it seldom amounted to more than a use of curving struts across the panel corners (32, 33)—or sometimes, in later cases, of straight ones, where the effect can be definitely rather unpleasing.

The filling-in of the walls, though local variations in method existed, was at first generally carried out by springing upright hazel wands into grooves notched in the timbers, and cross-weaving them with sticks or brushwood to form a close hurdling (21). The daub was applied to this wattle in the manner described in the last chapter; here again there were local varieties of consistence, that in Surrey being of marly clay mixed with chopped straw. The walls were finished with a coat of lime plaster or colour-wash, and the timbers were nearly always left their natural colour, weathering to a silvery grey that is infinitely preferable to the blackening now so popular. In later buildings, the plaster was generally brought exactly flush with the timbers; by an earlier (and possibly less attractive) practice it was sometimes recessed to a depth of about an inch.

An outstanding feature of the timber-framed houses of this period was the frequent projection, or jettying, of the upper storey. Sometimes this occurred at one end only, usually under a gable (30), but in earlier examples it was often followed around

26 ELMLEY CASTLE, WORCESTERSHIRE
Note the built-in chimney

25 EARDISLAND, HEREFORDSHIRE
Note the outbuilt chimney and bake-oven

27   A JETTIED FRONTAGE AT LEEDS, KENT, NOW
PLASTERED OVER

AN EXAMPLE OF JETTIED CONSTRUCTION AT LINGFIELD, SURREY
Drawn by W. Curtis Green, R.A.

all four walls. Various explanations have been offered for this convention: that it gave more room in the upper storeys, or that the recessed wall beneath received better protection from the weather. Some writers, however, have suggested that greater stability was thus obtained for the whole building on the cantilever principle, as the horizontal timbers, which were laid flat, were naturally " whippy," and a ceiling was apt to " dance " when there was much movement on the floor above.

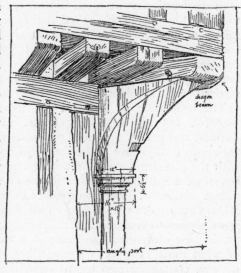

DETAIL OF A SURREY CORNER-POST
Drawn by W. Curtis Green, R.A.

Be it as it may, it was an arrangement that attracted the Tudor builder, and one in which he could find much scope for his natural ingenuity in woodwork. In the majority of such cases, the corner-posts at the angles were made from the bottom parts of trees turned upside down, so that the outward curve of the root, or spur, could help to support the projection (37). Heavy girder-beams were laid horizontally between these posts, which in jettied examples projected outwards some eighteen inches above the framing below (28); and use was generally made of another diagonal one from corner to corner, which was called the dragon-beam, and formed a familiar, if, for all its constructional desirability, somewhat unæsthetic interior feature, as it was invariably visible in the ground-floor ceiling.

Other horizontal beams were now connected longitudinally into this framework, and to these the floor joists were tenoned, sometimes splayed outward from the dragon-beam at increasing angles, and at others laid at right angles to the walls. Where jettying was employed, they were made to project the same distance over the ground-floor storey as the girder-beams, in earlier houses their ends being covered by a molded fascia-board (37). As time went on, however, this was abandoned, and the joist-ends were simply rounded off, as is the case with the majority of such timber-framed houses existing to-day (28). The framing of the upper storey could now follow that of the one beneath, the cill being laid along the ends of the overhanging timbers. Still later, it became customary to frame the two storeys together in one wall, braced by cross-girders, or summers—a practice which automatically spelt the doom of the jettied house.

The roof-space of these houses was generally large and wasteful, but the long deep lines, often undisturbed by dormers and gables, produced an attractive effect. Indeed, the varieties of silhouette to be found in cottage roofs, coupled with the pleasant texture or weathering property of the local covering, are still responsible for much of the charm of the village landscape. For convenience in roofing, cottages were seldom built more than one room thick, with a normal span of some sixteen to eighteen feet; but the countryman's inherent passion for outbuilding and extension have left few examples of what must have been the smallest type of two-storeyed cottage, containing two rooms only, the chamber above and the house-part beneath, under a roof either hipped or gable-ended. The building on of outshuts and lean-tos, over which

A SURREY COTTAGE, SHOWING THE JETTIED TIMBER
FRAMEWORK AND THE FINISHED BUILDING

Drawn by Alfred H. Powell.

the roof was brought down in steep catslides, of projecting
dormers under their own gablets, or of right-angle extensions
from the centre or ends of the original house, have all added
to the complexity of the cottage roofline. In the Suffolk
example sketched (*p.* 36), the twin outshuts have practically
the cubic space of the main building. Often a roof might
be gabled at one end over a jetty and hipped at the other, an
arrangement that found much favour in certain districts ;
but though the transverse gable was a feature of many farms
and yeomen's houses, particularly in the South-east, it made
only rare appearances in buildings of smaller stature.

Naturally, as the sixteenth century progressed, the status
of the wright improved with the rush of new building, and in
districts where timber-framing most flourished we find him
sometimes raised to the status of a capitalist on a quite substantial scale, as must have been the case with John Abel
(1577-1674), the " King's Carpenter," whose career coincided
with the commercial advancement of the Leominster district,
and whose yard had such fine individual buildings to its
credit as the market-halls at that town and at Ledbury, the
destroyed town-hall and the " Old House " at Hereford. The
epitaph on his tomb in Sarnesfield churchyard concludes :

> His house of clay could hold no longer ;
> May Heaven's joy frame him a stronger

—no doubt a reference to the part he played in the widespread substitution of timber-framing for wattle-and-daub in his district.

Under the new conditions, timbers were sawn to the
necessary scantlings in pits in the carpenters' yards ; after the
spoliation of Rochester Cathedral at the time of the Civil
War, for instance, we read that " they so far profaned this
place as to make use of it in the quality of a tippling place, as
well as dug several saw-pits, and the city joiners made frames
for houses in it." The practice of largely framing houses in
the yards, and then " rearing " them on the site with the help
of the populace, seems to have endured well into the
seventeenth century. Mr. Innocent * tells us, indeed, that
" the little flag which decorates the roof of a modern house
when it is ready for the slater is a survival from the days
when the setting up of the house was the ' rearing ' of crucks
or other heavy timbers by the neighbours " ; while frequently
in Southern England a green bush is still tied to the ridge
when the roof timbers are completely erected.

* *The Development of English Building Construction.*

29 JETTIED CONSTRUCTION IN A DERELICT
COTTAGE AT WARMISTER, GLOUCESTERSHIRE

28 JETTIED CONSTRUCTION AT BIGNOR,
SUSSEX

30   NEWENT, GLOUCESTERSHIRE

31   BRIDGNORTH, SHROPSHIRE
Note the brick filling of the originally recessed lower storey

These carpenters were often decorative craftsmen of some note, as can be gauged from the touches of detail that adorn many an old timber-framed cottage—the Gothic cusping or foliations of the gable " barge-boards," for instance, giving way, in Jacobean times, to a crude Renaissance ornament ; the deep and effective molding of the fascia-boards which at first concealed the joist-ends of the overhanging storeys ; the graceful treatment of timber mullions and window-frames ; and the stout panelling of many a door or partition wall. The heavy corner-posts and their spurs were sometimes singled out for special treatment, and were elaborately carved with figure-sculpture or floral designs.

The carpenter supplied not only the framework, but most of the fittings and ornamental detail for his houses. The dauber and the plasterer were responsible for the filling-in and finishing of the walls, while the roof covering was supplied by the thatcher, or, with increasing frequency as time went on, by the slater or the tiler. In the case of cottages, the use of stone-slates seems to have been somewhat restricted, though it must always have existed in the North and the Welsh Border district, and was certainly common in one well-defined district of Sussex around Horsham. Of early tiling we know little, as its local character has been destroyed by modern wholesale manufacture, but it is probable that in most cases the tiles were baked in the immediate neighbourhood where they were used. We can still admire their mellow colouring in many old cottages, and the beauty of texture resulting from their thickness, and unevenness of placing. But the whole subject of roof-coverings is treated separately and in detail in a later chapter.

As the sixteenth century progressed, the importance of the bricklayer began to increase for village building. Only a very minor use of brick had been made in the Middle Ages, owing to the fact that it was then almost entirely imported, and thus a " luxury " product ; but during the period under review it began to make an appearance as a filling for timber-framed walls, often laid in the familiar " herring-bone " pattern that is so attractive. It was towards the close of the sixteenth century, when chimneys began to be fitted more widely, not only to new but older cottages, that brick first found a permanent way into the village. In early days, as has been seen, the cottage fire was laid in a flat pan in the centre of the room, the smoke escaping as best it could through door and windows, or through an aperture in the roof such as is shown in the little cottage in the Grimani Breviary illustration (20). Later, when rooms came to be ceiled, the space under the roof was sometimes used as a "smoke chamber" for the concentration of the fumes, which, later still, with the first open hearths, was modified into a built-out flue above the overhanging canopy, often made of plastered wood or wattle-and-daub. From this to the brick or stone chimney was an obvious step in evolution. Then, as internal comfort increased, it became desirable to heat more than one room, and thus we often find two chimneys built on to a cottage, generally one at either end, or, as an alternative arrangement, a large chimney built up as a separate brick structure through the centre of the house, with fire-places opening on to the rooms on either hand. In such cases, great ingenuity was often shown in the structural management of joists, timbers and roof-coverings to accommodate it. On the outside, the grouping and silhouette of the stacks was nearly always charmingly handled, though in humbler cottages the brickwork was seldom molded or treated decoratively in any way, except for plain projecting courses. Occasionally, however, especially in Kent and East Anglia, the beauty and elaboration of the chimneys is out of all proportion to the modest little houses from which they rise in graceful clumps and clusters, delicately scored with moldings that the bricklayer formed roughly with the axe, and rubbed to the necessary finish with a float-stone. Sometimes, also, one finds a bake-oven built on to the base of an outside stack under a pyramidal or lean-to roof—an arrangement which can be most attractive (24, 25).

We have not so far touched directly on the subject of planning—perhaps a too formal word to use in connection with these little houses, whose growth to their present forms was often so haphazard and various. In the beginning, as has been seen, their arrangement was largely determined by the problem of roof construction, and the inability of the builders to cover them to a thickness of more than one span ; thus, the simplest type of two-roomed, two-storeyed cottage was most easily enlarged by building on an additional bay of similar construction, or by the addition of lean-tos and out-shuts over which the roof was carried down low, at one end of the house, at both ends, or in the form of a continuous series of sheds running the whole length of the back. Not many examples can remain of the original two-roomed house of two storeys, though a few are still to be found in Surrey,

A SUSSEX COTTAGE OF TWO STOREYS, SHOWING THE TIMBER
FRAMEWORK AND THE FINISHED BUILDING

Drawn by Alfred H. Powell.

and, built in stone, in the Cotswolds ; but there must be many in which this arrangement formed the basis of the present lay-out. The accompanying plan (*p.* 35) shows how considerably a simple Surrey cottage of two bays could be enlarged by outshuts. Other additions could be made, as has been seen, by right-angle extensions from the centre, or from one, or both, ends ; and when one considers a house enlarged in this way and then supplemented with further outshuts, the ramifications can be, as is easily imagined, extraordinary. Though the number of detached cottages that remain which were built as such, and have always been dwelt in by cottagers, is not now very great, continuous rows of cottages, dating from the great building periods, are still to be found more or less all over the country.

Brief reference must also be made to the well-defined plan of a certain type of yeoman's house, halfway, as it were, between a manor-house and a cottage, which was largely confined to the county of Kent and its borders, where some fifty or sixty examples are known to have existed within a small radius. This consisted of a central house-part, or hall, flanked by two slightly projecting wings, the roof being generally supported on the outside over the central recess by curved wind-braces. While originally the hall rose the whole height of the house, the wings each being divided into storeys containing offices and chambers, the obvious inconvenience of this arrangement generally led to the central portion being itself subdivided during the sixteenth century or later ; and it is common to find one of the old roof king-posts embedded in an upper partition wall. Good examples of this type of plan are to be seen at Pattenden, Goudhurst, Shorne, Stonehill, Chiddingly and other Kentish places, with an occasional appearance as far afield as Bignor in Sussex (28, 32) and Newport in Essex. A modified form consisted of a house-part flanked by a single wing of two storeys—an arrangement similar in principle to that of the dwelling-house of the Yorkshire " coit " described in the last chapter (*p.* 21).

As has been seen, brick was always used to some extent as a filling for timber-framed walls, a practice known as " brick-nogging," which was more particularly found in East Anglia. Much ingenuity was shown in the arrangement of the small, rich-toned bricks, which could be laid diagonally, chequer-wise, or in the pleasant herring-bone fashion. Flints could also be used where a supply was available, as in some old West Sussex cottages ; the effective panelling or diapering

32 A COTTAGE OF KENTISH YEOMAN TYPE, WITH RECESSED
CENTRE, AT BIGNOR, SUSSEX

33 FOURTEENTH-CENTURY HALF-TIMBER AT THE PRIEST'S
HOUSE, ALFRISTON, SUSSEX

34 KIDMORE END, ~~BERKSHIRE~~ *OXON.*

35 BLEWBURY, BERKSHIRE

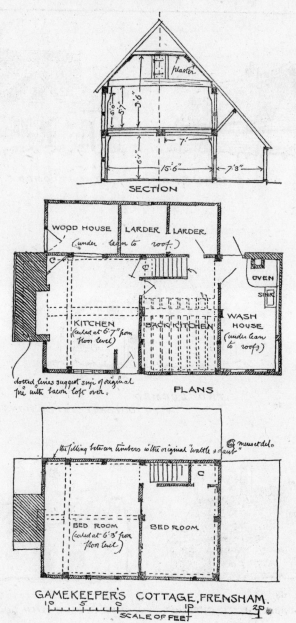

SECTION

PLANS

GAMEKEEPER'S COTTAGE, FRENSHAM.

ENLARGEMENT BY OUTSHUTS IN A SURREY COTTAGE

Drawn by W. Curtis Green, R.A.

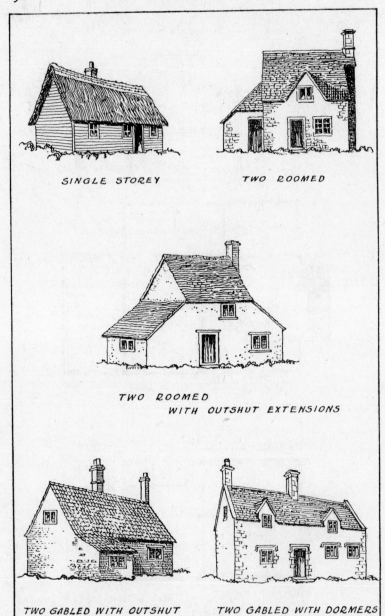

SINGLE STOREY

TWO ROOMED

TWO ROOMED
WITH OUTSHUT EXTENSIONS

TWO GABLED WITH OUTSHUT

TWO GABLED WITH DORMERS

COTTAGE PROFILES

Stifford, Essex

Farnham, Suffolk

Typical : Central-East Suffolk

Ablington, Gloucestershire

Stanton, Gloucestershire

TWO GABLED WITH
COMPLETE BACK EXTENSION

GABLE AND ONE HIP
OVER OUTSHUT

DOUBLE HIPPED

ONE LATERAL GABLE

TWO LATERAL GABLES

COTTAGE PROFILES

Typical : founded on a Cottage
    at Normandy, Surrey

Near Shere, Surrey

Swanton Street, Kent

Shamley Green, Surrey

Little Dunmow, Essex

G

37

of these with brickwork, rare in timber-framed walls, is a subject which will be given more prominence in a later chapter. The disadvantage of this type of filling, however, was that bricks or flints could not be properly bonded into the timbers unless the latter were keyed; while even with the ordinary wattle-and-daub filling there was an inevitable shrinkage as the clay dried.

It will be seen later that the course of structural decay has often resulted in completely disguising what are, beneath the tiles, boards or plaster, ordinary timber-framed cottages. Just occasionally we find a house of this type that has been entirely cased without at a later date with brick or stone, but more often such casing was reserved for the lower storey only, where, with a jettied building, it had the effect of filling in the recess and producing a flush line (31). In larger houses, structural defects could be remedied by interior panelling or tapestries, but the cottager had to resort to the local material most easily available for keeping his home dry and sound. These little structures were of necessity utilitarian, and in their slowly perfected use of local resources lies much of their charm. Here and there a carved barge-board or corner-post, a molded chimney or a graceful oriel speak of a man's desire to distinguish his home out of the crowd; but the majority reflect in their sturdy simplicity little more than the bare domestic requirements of the old-time rural worker. As such it is fitting that they should be preserved, even though to-day we have far over-reached those modest standards of household comfort.

IV

REGIONAL CHARACTERISTICS OF THE TIMBER-FRAMED COTTAGE

It is by no means easy to determine the influence of local types of building on cottage half-timber, and there is need for a comprehensive regional survey to be carried out, in which these differences can be noted, collated and systematised. The work, of course, is of the plainest, the materials, even though original, are of an inexpensive type, and the craftsmanship, though usually sound, is of the simplest and most straightforward. Generally, it is probable that the differences in the dates of building are stronger and more definitely marked than those attributable to the influence of the local building tradition; the period factor overweighs the place factor, though this must not be unduly stressed. It is interesting to see how bodies of craftsmen, working independently in different parts of the country according to well-established methods, probably largely by rule of thumb and rather haphazardly, produced work which is not so very different from the Marches of Wales to the coast of Suffolk, from the rolling country of Leicestershire to the English Channel. Indeed, it is easier to write of the unity than of the diversity of half-timber buildings, and such differences as are discernible on a limited survey are chiefly in finishing, methods of filling, etc., rather than in the actual construction.

Crucks, which are found to the West and North of the Humber-Severn line, as has been mentioned (*p.* 16), remind us that primitive work of early form has still to be reckoned with, if slightly, in English building, and that there has been a definite method of timber building practised in England for some six centuries back. Generally speaking, the earlier work is denoted by the closer spacing of the timbers, but this is by no means an infallible guide, though usually correct; indeed, it is difficult to generalise in any remarks of this kind, because the individual builder unconsciously went against any rule and produced an individual result.

Regarded as a whole, this half-timber building is a heritage by no means to be despised. But it represents the plainest, simplest and occasionally the roughest version—one would hesitate to call it a poor relation—of the splendid achievement of English timber building, one of the greatest triumphs of English craftsmanship, though, with that peculiar unseeing perversity which is so typical, one of the least understood or appreciated.

Much of the heritage of medieval craftsmanship in wood has been spared to us in our churches, but it is only of recent years that we have begun to gauge something of its richness and its splendour. The domestic work, dating mostly from the fifteenth to the seventeenth century, was equally magnificent, but only scattered fragments of it remain. The glory of English timber house-building has largely passed in the wanton and insensate destruction of the nineteenth century, which commercialism and red tape in the twentieth are doing their best to carry on. Those who wish to realise the grandeur of which we have been bereft must study the priceless records set down for all time in John C. Buckler's hundreds of careful drawings in the British Museum.

It is not for us, in this brief and cursory account, to attempt even the barest note on half-timber work in other countries. And yet, even if the English work is to be regarded as of independent and indigenous growth, it is but a little insular flowering of a plant which has other stems and blossoms. The *châlets* and farm buildings of the Swiss and other Alpine peoples are tremendous structures entirely in timber, like that other very individual manifestation, the mast churches of Norway. More nearly akin to our own buildings are the many-storied half-timber houses of Western Germany and Alsace—the towering structures of Nuremberg, Rothenburg and their fellows. But some of the most charming examples are to be found in the villages dotted about the Alsatian plain from Strasbourg and Colmar to the wooded Vosges escarpment. The timber-work of these two principal Alsatian cities will hold its own easily with that of the more famous German show-places ; but in the compactly built streets of such places as Ingolsheim, Geispolsheim, Innenheim, Krautergersheim and above all Bläsheim, there are massively built three-sided farmsteads and barns, of half-timber throughout and forming a quadrangle with the street. They are of simple bold design and well-judged construction, forming a unified whole. Mixed among these are smaller dwellings, probably for farm workers, of plain rectangular shape, which differ not essentially from the timber village building of Herefordshire. This art merits to be better known and more appreciatively studied ; it is a first cousin of those farms and cottages of which we may well be legitimately proud. And if on the Other Side the Alsatian designers and carpenters have met John Abel

36 POST-AND-PAN WORK AT ASTON CANTLOW,
WARWICKSHIRE

37 MOLDED CORNER-POST AND FASCIA-BOARD IN A FIFTEENTH-
CENTURY COTTAGE ROW AT CLAVERING, ESSEX

38 SHACKLEFORD, SURREY

39 EASEBOURNE, WEST SUSSEX

and his fellow craftsmen, we may rest assured that they have found a pleasant fellowship of mutual esteem in the discussion and comparison of the tasks which they so rejoicingly fulfilled.

A rough classification of the chief divisions of timber cottage building is suggested as follows, though it must be understood that these areas shade very much into each other, and there is seldom any hard-and-fast demarcation :—

1. East Anglia : Suffolk, Essex, Cambridgeshire and Huntingdonshire.
2. Southern :

> (*a*) North of Thames—Hertfordshire, Buckinghamshire and Bedfordshire.
> (*b*) South-east of Thames—Kent, Sussex and Surrey.
> (*c*) Central South to West—Hampshire, Berkshire, South Oxfordshire and Wiltshire, with the Gloucestershire Vale as a connecting link with Division 3.

3. Midlands and Welsh Border : Warwickshire, Worcestershire, Herefordshire, Shropshire and Cheshire.

A certain amount of timber building occurs in Leicestershire, Nottinghamshire, Lancashire, etc., but only sparsely scattered among the prevailing stone and brick.

1. East Anglia

For our present purposes East Anglia must be regarded as consisting of Suffolk and Essex, with the adjacent counties of Huntingdonshire and Cambridgeshire. Norfolk never indulged very much in timber building, but preferred to work in various combinations of brick and flint, and occasionally mud plastered.

The area under consideration is as fine a district of timber as the South-east itself, but this does not leap to the eye to anything like the same extent, because it has been decreed that the achievements of its fine traditional craftsmanship shall be largely veiled behind plaster. If the people of East Anglia have chosen to hide their timber craftsmanship behind this comely coat, who shall gainsay or revile them ? The thatched or tiled houses, with their white or tinted plaster, are in entire accord with the pastoral landscape, and in certain areas the East Anglian villages are among the finest examples of minor domestic work in England, a precious heritage though not even a perfervid journalist could term them "imperishable," seeing that they are being torn from us piecemeal by the exactions of so-called reformers.

Even the humble types of cottage building in this eastern province are instinct with that tradition of well-finished craftsmanship which is native to the district, and in these quiet buildings it finds expression as definitely, though in a less intense degree, as in the splendour of craftsmanship of the great churches. The richest timber-work in East Anglia is found, as might be expected, in the larger houses—fine buildings which owe their origin largely to the industrial phase through which the district passed between the fifteenth and seventeenth centuries, which has left its mark in weavers' houses at Lavenham, Kersey and elsewhere, and in the old factories and maltings found in such places as Dedham, Saffron Walden and Woodbridge.

There are a fair number of examples of the earlier post-and-pan work, such as the cottages in the churchyard at Cockfield; and the long rows of closely timbered houses at Bildeston, Suffolk, are particularly fine. A special variety of East Anglian filling is the one layer of bricks between the posts, set at angles, as at Laxfield and Fressingfield. Larger examples have the picturesque herring-bone brick patterns, but the filling is often plastered flush with the timbering. Often the timbers are spaced midway between the post-and-pan work and the wider framing of the South-east and the Midlands—in fact, the typical example of East Anglia is a gable of this type incorporating two curved braces.

Overhanging storeys are frequent, either on gables or sides of houses, and occasionally on both, usually with the rounded ends of the timbers showing. Corner-posts, not of course of elaborate carving, occur on cottages (37), and sometimes the East Anglian resorted to additional brackets for further strengthening. Now and then cottages show the original East Anglian tradition in Tudor doorways, but more often there is a neat later hood of inverted V shape. Porches are comparatively rare in cottage building, but there are occasional later doorheads and sash windows. The finished strength of East Anglian craftsmanship is shown in some pleasant oriels and bays, with good brackets and finials, and in the fine brick chimneys. Some windows have shutters which punctuate pleasantly the expanses of tinted plaster. An excellent example of the better type of East Anglian cottage building, with an oriel under the first storey, was to be seen at Stanstead, near

Long Melford, dated 1653 and burnt in 1910; it is illustrated in Oliver's *Old Cottages of East Anglia*, plate 49. The district loved the gable, and the steep high-pitched one at that, and the two-gabled cottage is so much the rule that a hipped

IN THE VILLAGE STREET, HINXTON, CAMBRIDGESHIRE
Drawn by Sydney R. Jones.

roof, single or double, produces a mild feeling of surprise. The mansard roof occurs locally in Cambridgeshire cottages (137) and to a slight extent elsewhere in East Anglia.

2. THE SOUTH

The South-eastern area is not, like its opposite number, the South-west, a well-defined or self-contained district. The three counties south of the Thames form a projecting peninsula, but north of the river, Hertfordshire, Buckinghamshire and Bedfordshire shade on the one hand into East Anglia and abut on the Cotswolds on the other. To the west of the South-east projection, Hampshire, Berkshire, South Oxfordshire, Wiltshire and the vale country of Gloucestershire connect to the north with the Midlands and Welsh Border country. This somewhat heterogeneous district will for convenience be considered as a whole, for there is no space to attempt a detailed survey of the local divergencies, which are not very striking.

Half-timber cottage building is abundant throughout the whole area, but especially in the three South-eastern counties, where, as has been pointed out, numerous local industries, which have since died out, tended to raise considerably the standard of lesser domestic building, backed of course by an abundant supply of the diversified local materials which the varied geology of the district placed at the builders' disposal.

The South-eastern counties are the home of a splendid type of large farmstead, which as it occurs (*e.g.*) round Ockley and Shamley Green is among the finest indigenous products of the smaller English house. These dwellings have largely been turned into country residences, a fate that frequently overtakes this type of house in recent days, especially in the Cotswolds. In Kent there is the indigenous type of yeoman's house with a central hall, originally open to the roof, recessed in the centre between two projecting overhanging wings. There is a small example of this type at Bignor, Sussex (28, 32), which has been somewhat restored, and its present condition shows a remarkable variety of brick-and-flint fillings. The Six Bells Inn at Hollingbourne was one of the most charming of this type, but it has unfortunately been destroyed by fire. The majority have the central hall floored over, a process of conversion dating in some cases as far back as the sixteenth century. Few remain in their original condition, though some, like Stoneacre in the parish of Otham, have been reconverted to their original form.

The style of timber-framing is, throughout the district under consideration, plain, workmanlike and straightforward. It is only in larger houses, such as Middle House, Mayfield and Great Tangley Manor, that the South-eastern timber craftsman proved that he could vie with his Cheshire cousin in elaboration if he let himself go. The craftsmanship standard is particularly high, but it is sometimes not easy to know whether a row of old cottages, especially in Kent, may not be the remains of, say, a medieval cloth factory. Similarly, it can perhaps scarcely be claimed that the general run of pleasant small houses in such a town as Rye are of cottage status.

Generally, the timbering of the genuine cottage is somewhat

40 NEAR FITTLEWORTH, WEST SUSSEX

41 HARDHAM, WEST SUSSEX

42 WEST HAGBOURNE, BERKSHIRE

casual and fortuitous, and pieces of different spacing occur on the same building. The fine gabled row at Aldbury, Hertford-shire, by the stocks, is a striking example of this. There is a good deal of post-and-pan work, but mostly in the larger farmhouses dating from the latter half of the fifteenth century, as at Stonehill, Chiddingly. The timber spacing cannot be taken as an infallible guide to the date of the cottage, because the little fourteenth-century vicarage in the churchyard at Alfriston (33) is irregularly, but on the whole fairly widely, spaced, and this type is also found on a curved range of early work with overhanging storey at the side of the Crown Inn, Chiddingfold. Overhanging work is fairly common, some-times on one side, sometimes the whole way round, while occasionally, as in East Anglia, extra timber brackets help to support the upper storey, as in a well-proportioned example at Byworth, near Petworth. Generally, the cottages have fairly wide spacing, with occasional straight or slightly curved diagonal bracing, which may occur anywhere with apparent casualness in the upper storey ; less commonly these diagonal braces will rather awkwardly run through from the floor to the eaves.

Much of the timber-work has the filling plastered flush ; sometimes the whole of a front will be white- or colour-washed over the timbering and filling alike (42). Brick filling is fre-quently used, sometimes in herring-bone, and it can often be seen by the different colours and variety of bricks that the filling between a number of the timber spaces has been renewed at different times and in divers manners. In the chalk Bourne Valley near Andover, where Hampshire, Berkshire and Wilt-shire meet, a filling occurs of alternate layers of brick and flint ; it is perhaps a Wiltshire Downland form.

Plastering, weatherboarding and tilehanging have, as will be seen, been freely used and hereabouts two of these weatherproofing methods may be found on the same building, all helping to give that variety of texture which is one of the greatest charms of the district. The typical small Surrey cottage has a gable at one end, abutting against the chimney, and the roof coming down straight over the outshut at the other (p. 37). The typical larger house in Kent, as in the fine example at Swanton Street (p. 37) is hipped at both ends.

Kent has, with its fine craftsmanship tradition, a good range of oriel windows and well-designed and appropriate detail (finials, barge-boards, etc.) as in the fine row at Bidden-den and some examples at Canterbury, which rival work of this type in East Anglia. Oriels occur also in the Petworth and Pulborough district of Sussex.

Wiltshire has building styles as diversified as its own geology ; some of these fall to be dealt with in other sections. Its half-timber work is consequently not very much to the fore, though examples, mixed with conglomerate stone, brick and flint, occur among the downland villages, and those at the foot of the hills. Indeed, half-timber work is found in most Wiltshire villages away from the limestone area ; in lonely pockets among the downland spurs, resting in rustic placidity in the hamlets of the lush green river valleys, and scattered singly or in groups through the vale country. In Dorset, however, timber building is rare ; the pleasant thatched townships of its extensive chalk area are chiefly plastered or cob, and stone with thatch is the note of the western districts. On the other hand, Hampshire, Berkshire, and the vale country of Gloucestershire form a wide district in which there is a considerable amount of half-timber cottage work, usually roofed with thatch (9, 18, 136). There is little that is remarkable about the details of such building, but on the other hand there is no doubt that it produces a harmonious and pleasant effect which has commended it to artists in search of the pretty and picturesque for generations (30, 34-5, 43). Pleasantly placed by the side of a lane amid orchards or approached by a flight of rough stone steps as they stand perched on the top of a bank, there is no doubt that these dwellings represent quite typically what the over-seas exile, the foreigner and those immured in towns regard as the old English cottage. Their thatch curves in a wavy line or is cut back sharply over the small windows set round the eaves. They are surrounded by gardens gay with flowers in all the leafy months, and it would seem churlish with all this charm to obtrude a doubt as to how far their roofs are free from leaks, their rooms warm in the winter and their sanitation removed from the unspeakable.

3. THE MIDLANDS AND THE WELSH BORDER

Black-and-white farms and cottages fit very pleasantly into the green and smiling landscape of the Midlands and Welsh Border ; they take their place naturally with the undulating fields of red earth and the hop-gardens, and stand sedately under the wooded ridges. By the Welsh Border they are normal throughout the district, but the chief area of concentration is west of Leominster, with Weobley, chiefly, of course, composed of larger houses, Eardisland, Pembridge, Dilwyn and Wellington. It is interesting that so much timbering occurs in a district of diversified rock formations of hard type, where building-stone of a sort was ever readily obtainable; it emphasises how firmly rooted was the timber-building tradition. A grim kind of stone cottage of a featureless type, however, occurs in the hilly country of South Shropshire, and there is a good deal of later brick throughout Worcestershire. Some of the most charming cottages in half-timber occur in the Severn and Avon valleys stretching to the foot of the Cotswold escarpment, as Ashton-under-Hill (43), and there are no pleasanter villages in England than Elmley Castle (26), Great and Little Comberton and Cleeve Prior.

In the counties under review, Warwickshire, Worcestershire, Herefordshire, Shropshire and Cheshire, post-and-pan work is comparatively rare, and when found usually occurs in larger domestic buildings or mills, though a fairly large number of cruck-built cottages have survived to remind us that work of primitive type is still to be found in rural houses. Examples in Herefordshire are to be found at Leinthall Starkes, Eardisley, Kinnersley, Putley, Tarrington, Much Marcle, even in Hereford itself, usually with later side-walls. The typical Midland cottage is timber-framed in squares, or divisions slightly higher than they are broad, usually plastered flush with the timbers, which are painted black, thus giving the well-known black-and-white or "magpie" effect. Fillings of rosy brick are not unknown, but usually on larger houses.

In the simple construction adopted, one square of the timbering is filled by each of the windows and two by the doors (5, 127), though of course this practice is subject to a large number of irregularities and exceptions. The timber-framing serves for window-frame. Curved or straight diagonal bracing is not common, and the elaborate patterning found in larger houses is usually absent in cottages, though at Alderley, Cheshire, there are one or two examples of pleasing chequerwork timbering. We look vainly among the cottages for even the simple lozenge-like patterns found at Dodmore Farm, near Ludlow, or the diagonal design of the charming destroyed and surviving buildings at Craven Arms; yet this work becomes irritating in the vast range of Pitchford Hall. The craftsman showed his hand in the striking patterning of the curious little Buttas Falconry. Windows are usually small, and often the only upper window is in the side gable near the chimney. Two gables are much more common than the hips of the South-east, though the roof is sometimes hipped back when covered with thatch. Generally, the construction and effect is much more fortuitous, haphazard and casual than the more finished and fully worked-out traditional craftsmanship of Kent and Surrey buildings.

If the timber itself is of the plain grid type, there is much

MARSTON SICCA, GLOUCESTERSHIRE

Drawn by Sydney R. Jones.

variety of patterns in the gable-ends (43-4); the characteristic West Midland pattern being an intersecting double V, as seen at Pembridge (127). Against the gable-ends are usually placed the chimneys, made frequently of great size, in rubble stone in the lower part (25), often in several diminishing stages, with a fairly slender straight stack in brick, generally with plain copings. Near the chimney often protrudes a little bake-oven, frequently circular and tiled, or rounded at the edges, with a small lean-to roof all to itself (25).

The cottages are frequently placed in a scattered series in the villages or hamlets, as in such places as Eardisland, Kings-

43 ASHTON-UNDER-HILL, GLOUCESTERSHIRE

44 TROTSHILL, WORCESTERSHIRE

land, Orleton and many another.   They are also found singly
or in threes and fours by the sides of lanes, and occasionally
occur isolated high on the hill-sides, as at Stockton Hill above
the Golden Valley.   Sometimes they are of the small two- or
four-roomed type, but changing conditions of the country
have caused the ebbing of the human tide that once filled
them, so that they stand empty and every year fall more
desolately into ruin.   Such little houses are found forlorn
above Yatton near Wigmore, on Bircher Common and high
in the Downton hills of Bringewood Chase.   They are a
quite typical product of a country that has been purely
agricultural.   As a rule they have been little meddled with,
but there can be a painful fussy effect after injudicious making-
over in the nineteenth century, as in rows at Ombersley and
Eardisland.

H

V

THE COB COTTAGE

It has been seen that the peasant's cote of the Middle Ages was often built of mud, without a supporting timber framework. This type of walling remained in use throughout the great periods of cottage building, being known variously as " clom," " clob " or, of more recent years, " cob "—its most common name to-day. It was an economical and, if well carried out, surprisingly durable form of building that for long found favour in almost every part of the land, though its survival is now largely restricted to the South-western counties, particularly Devon, where its combination with thatch lends an individual and charming character to many an old village. Mr. Innocent has suggested* that in the beginning mud, or cob, was used as an intermediate filling between double wattlework walls, and that when the wattle covering decayed, it was found that the building remained sound without its support. Be it as it may, it is known that mud walls were in use for London houses as early as 1212, and that from distant times cottages have existed in many parts of the country which were built by their occupants of the roadscrapings which were found to provide so useful a consistence, this having been still the practice in the Banbury district of Oxfordshire as late as the middle of the last century, where the mud walls were of such durability that it was almost impossible to demolish them with picks.

As a protection against damp and vermin, cob walls, particularly in Devon, were often built on a low stone foundation, over which they were made to project about 1½ inches. The first layer would be built some 2½ feet high around this foundation, to a thickness of about 2 feet, the only implements used being a dungfork and a kind of shallow shovel known as a cob-parer. Since the material was very wet and soft at the time of use, about a week had to be allowed for drying (according to the time of year) before building up the next layer—so that cob-building was of necessity a lengthy undertaking. Sometimes, in uncertain weather, a coping of thatch would be used as a temporary protection for unfinished walls (as was also the case for the ashlar masonry of the Middle Ages), thus giving rise to the Devonshire proverb, " that all cob wants is a good hat and a good pair of shoes "—*i.e.* a thatch coping and a stone foundation. During building, one

* *The Development of English Building Construction.*

46 COB AND THATCH AT ITS TIDIEST: Minehead Old Village,
Somerset

47 OLD COB AND THATCH, LUSTLEIGH, DEVON

48 OLD COB AND COBBLES, LUSTLEIGH, DEVON

49 "ALL COB NEEDS IS A GOOD HAT AND A GOOD PAIR
OF SHOES": Dunsford, Devon

workman probably stood on the wall to tread it down, while another threw on the cob, the woodwork, such as door-lintels, window-frames or beams to carry a second storey, being fitted into the walls as construction proceeded. To avoid cracking—always the major enemy of cob-building—the corners of the houses were nearly always rounded off, as may still be seen with pleasant effect in many West Country cottages (46, 50).

In the days before far-reaching specialisation of life, build-ing regulations and trade union restrictions, it was of frequent occurrence for a rustic bridegroom-elect to erect his cob cottage with his own hands. The leisurely process was carried out in a leisurely way, but the result attained was durable, and the accommodation, if limited, was comfortably warm and dry. In her *Devonshire Idylls*, Miss Macneil recounts how a young labourer, with some help from his father-in-law-elect, raised the cob walls of the cottage for his bride, and roofed it with a coat of thatch. There he dwelt in comfort till his death, and his widow continued to inhabit it till she followed him many years after.

The consistence of the cob varied in different parts of the country with the local resources. Where chalk was available, this was always considered a valuable ingredient, as in parts of Dorset, where cob-building was described as he remembered it by Thomas Hardy in a letter to *The Times* (11th March 1927) :

What was called mud-wall was really a composition of chalk, clay and straw—essentially unbaked brick. This was mixed up into a sort of dough-pudding close to where the cottage was to be built. The mixing was performed by treading and shovelling—women sometimes being called in to tread—and the straw was added to bind the mass together. . . . It was then thrown by pitchforks on to the wall, where it was trodden down to a thickness of about two feet, till a rise of about three feet had been reached. This was left to settle for a day or two. . . .

Mr. Addy has described the composition of the mud walls of an old cottage which he examined at Great Hartfield in East Yorkshire :*.

The walls are built of layers of mud and straw which vary from five to seven inches in thickness, no vertical joints being visible. On the top of each layer is a thin covering of straw, with the ends of the straws pointing outwards, as in a corn stack. The way in which mud walls were built is remembered in the neighbourhood. A quantity of mud was mixed with straw, and the foundation laid with this mixture. Straw was then laid across the top, whilst the

* *The Evolution of the English House.*

mud was wet, and the whole was left to dry and harden in the sun. As soon as the first layer was dry, another layer was put on, so that the process was rather a slow one. Finally the roof was thatched, and the projecting ends of straws trimmed off the walls. Such mud walls are very hard and durable, and their composition resembles that of sun-burnt bricks.

It was usual, as is seen from these cases, to mix straw or stubble with the mud to bind it together, a process known as " tempering," though heath was used as a substitute in the sandy districts of Dorset. In Cornwall, Mr. Innocent tells us, " cob was composed of two loads of clay to one load of shilf, that is, broken slate in small pieces such as is used for mending roads, barley straw being added afterwards." In Buckinghamshire, " the walls were built of a kind of white clay called ' witchit ' found about eighteen inches below the surface of the ground." Further local varieties must always have existed, but it was generally considered preferable, even where the material was scarce, to use ground-up chalk for the finishing-coat, or " rough-cast," though loam, gravel and sand were also employed for this purpose in the heathy parts of Dorset.

The laboriousness of cob-building, and the structural limitations it imposed, restricted its use almost entirely to buildings of humbler stature, such as cottages and farm-ranges, for which it always seems appropriate. Cob cottages are invariably whitewashed or colour-washed over, except, perhaps, for a tarred plinth, and roofed with thatch brought down low over the eaves and carried in scallops around the diminutive upper windows. This roofing, from an aesthetic point of view, combines ideally with the walls, which, if kept in good repair, and clean, give an impression of neat simplicity that is pleasantly in keeping with the West Country setting. Most cob cottages that survive are to be found in the counties of Wiltshire, Somerset, Dorset and Devon, with a sprinkling as far afield as Hampshire and Berkshire ; but Devon remains pre-eminently the county of the cob village, the smoothly mingling lines of walls and roofs broken only by the tapering height of the chimneys outbuilt at the ends of the little houses. It seems a pity that legislation has nowadays almost precluded the use of this material, so harmonious with any country background, for modern housing purposes, for its survival is the test of its durability, not only in cottages, but in farm-buildings, and those thatched and gracefully curving farmyard walls which add charm to so many a West Country lane.

50 A COB CORNER OF DEVON

51 TYPICAL DORSET MASONRY: Springhead

VI

THE STONE-BUILT COTTAGE

Stone cottages are now to be found in most districts where the material is easily quarried, but its employment for minor buildings is seldom of much antiquity. While there was always some use of cob, wood-and-wattle remained the almost universal vernacular for cottage building until well into the seventeenth century, by which time the destruction of the forests had so raised the price of timber that, for the first time, stone could compete with it for such modest purposes. Throughout the whole great northern zone which we now associate with stone, wood-and-wattle had, until then, been preponderantly in use, even now surviving incongruously here and there among the later stone walls of some Yorkshire and Lancashire villages. In Cornwall, until quite recently, cob was often preferred to the surface granite so abundant there, though cottages built of large, unhewn granite boulders, put together without mortar, had also existed from early times (53).

In the roughest and earliest masonry used for minor buildings the stones were seldom quarried; a sufficient supply generally existed on the surface of the ground, as in Donegal to-day, or could be extracted from the beds of rivers and from boulder clay. The rudimentary mason, if such he can be called, not only built the walls but collected the boulders and broke them up. We can admire his ingenuity in fitting together pieces of different shape and size in examples of dry masonry still in use about the country, such as the field-walls of the Cotswolds and the Yorkshire moors, from which it should be almost impossible to pull any one stone out of place. In most mountain and moorland districts, such as Dartmoor, the Isle of Man, North Wales and the Scottish Highlands, old cottages are still commonly to be seen which were built in this manner of great stones fitted together to a thickness of two feet or more, perhaps plastered or whitewashed over, and covered either with thick stone-slates, or a thatch that might also envelop the meagre chimneys (83). Though adhesive mortar was seldom used in their walls, the stones were often bedded in earth beaten up with water, but generally unmixed with lime. Lime, clay and even cow-dung were used in mortar only when a more advanced masonry called for a sticky consistence, the purpose of this bedding being rather to keep out draughts and damp than to provide a permanent bonding. Alternatively, the gaps between the boulders could be filled in with small stones or rubble.

Beyond such mountain and moorland districts, where the weather generally necessitated a stouter protection than wood-and-wattle could provide, and where in any case the supply of loose stone probably exceeded that of timber, stone was used only to a negligible extent for cottage building until the close of the sixteenth century, and then only, as in the Cotswolds, where a ready supply was at hand for quarrying. In such cases, the character of the masonry largely depended on the nature of the local product, and the form in which it came from the quarry. The carefully coursed and dressed " ashlar " of more ambitious buildings was rare to the point of non-existence in cottages, but the village builder, who must generally have had the stonework of a church or manor-house for a model, was sometimes able to produce walls that formed an effective compromise between the rougher types of masonry and a freestone finish. Particularly where the stone was obtainable in large block, as was often the case in Yorkshire and the North, he could construct walls of roughly squared stones of almost equal size, with level joints and perhaps some attempt at coursing (65), which were usually left dry on the outside and filled internally with rubble, sand or clay. Where large blocks were rare, however, they were used only for window-dressings and quoins, the remainder of the walls being filled in with random rubble, as with many Cotswold cottages (75). In other cottages of the Limestone Belt, where the material came out in thin, slaty and almost uniform layers, a rough natural coursing was automatically obtained ; but in the least pretentious examples all over the country, the stones were simply built into the walls higgledy-piggledy, large and small, and no attempt was made at dressing beyond the knocking off of projections with a hammer and the rough scabbling of angles with an axe (51).

Stone walls were generally built to a thickness of between eighteen inches and two feet, but, where filled internally with rubble or small stones, their sturdy appearance was apt to belie their powers of resistance to damp and cold, especially when, as was often the case, there were no foundations, and the flagstones of the floor rested directly upon the ground. In their planning and arrangement, these cottages were subject to much the same limitations as those of wood-and-wattle, mainly from the inability of the builders to roof them to a thickness of more than one room. Thus, enlargement was

52 A PRIMITIVE GRANITE ROW, DARTMOOR

53 BOULDER GRANITE MASONRY AT SENNEN, CORNWALL

54 LITTLE BARRINGTON, OXON

55 NETHER WESTCOTE, OXON

THE DETACHED COTSWOLD COTTAGE AT ITS BEST

generally effected by outbuilding, by a right-angle projection, or by adding further bays, to arrive eventually, perhaps, at the cottage-row so well adapted to stone building, of which a perfect example has been preserved for the nation in Arlington Row at Bibury in the Cotswolds (75, 76). It was common practice to build up the gable-ends solid to carry the roof-tree, but occasionally, as in the Broadway cottage illustrated (58), a wooden cill was inserted along the top of the end wall from which the gable was constructed of wood-and-wattle. Stone-slates were the most frequent and appropriate covering for stone houses, but in both respects thatch often ran them close, while in some districts, as will be seen later, there was much use of red pantiles.

Stone cottages were invariably built from the product of a near-by quarry, and it is to their resultant variety in masonry technique, colour, texture, and so on, that they owe the intensely local character that is much of their charm. Though nearly always appropriate to their surroundings, it must be admitted that, æsthetically, they seldom rise beyond an average of sturdy seemliness, save in a few well-defined districts, chief among them the diagonal Limestone Belt running from Dorset to Lincolnshire, and culminating in Cotswold. Cotswold forms, indeed, a small architectural world of its own, the best productions of which belong to a period of little more than a hundred years, roughly from 1580 to 1690. Two important factors influenced their evolution : the wool prosperity of the district at the time, when the wold formed a vast sheepwalk, and the breeding of sheep and production of wool occupied practically every town and village to its profit ; and the presence throughout the uplands of a generous supply of limestone within a few feet of the surface, which, despite variations in its quarried form, provided an ideal building medium both as to texture and weathering property, from the golden-brown of the newly quarried block to the tinged and lichened grey of the seasoned product. The same style was employed for manor-houses, market-halls, farm-buildings and cottages, varying in richness according to the building's scale but always displaying the fundamental characteristics of strength, simplicity and suitability to purpose. Though at first retaining some vestiges of the Perpendicular of the preceding century, it quickly developed on its own lines, needing but slight modification, as time went on, to adapt itself in the detail to the developing course of Renaissance design.

These were stone houses through and through, produced by local masons to suit local conditions and the requirements of local people. The majority of cottages were built as self-contained units; the accompanying plans show the arrangement of typical examples of one and two cells. In the latter case, the stairs, as was usual, ascended from the centre of the house straight into the master's bedroom; in early cottages they might have been of stone on a circular plan around a central newel, but as time went on a similar structure in oak would probably have been preferred.

A COTSWOLD COTTAGE OF ONE CELL

A feature of the interiors was their compactness, and in most cases, let it be admitted, their lack of convenience. No store-cupboards, larders, sculleries or sanitary offices were provided for

A COTTAGE HEARTH OF COTSWOLD TYPE, MARSTON MAGNA, SOMERSET

Drawn by Sydney R. Jones.

in the plan, though a round bake-oven was nearly always incorporated as shown, opening out of one of the fireplaces. These latter, generally remarkably capacious in comparison with the little rooms they heated, would be spanned either by a four-centred stone arch or an oak lintel, and would contain, hollowed out of the stone on either hand, the small ingle-seats always so dear to the English villager. Partition walls were

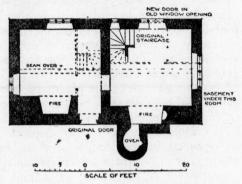

A COTSWOLD COTTAGE OF TWO CELLS

made of oak framing, and the floors were either carried on joists from wall to wall, or rested on great beams placed centrally across the rooms, without relation, however, to the positions of doors, fireplaces or windows. The ground floors were usually stone-flagged.

DORMER-GABLES AT WINSON, IN THE COLN VALLEY, GLOUCESTERSHIRE

Drawn by Sydney R. Jones.

On the outside, one of the most familiar Cotswold features was the dormer window. This was necessitated by the lack of height of the walls, which in cottages seldom rose more than fifteen feet from ground to eaves, that is to say, only about four feet above the level of the upper floor. There was thus obviously no room for upper windows under the eaves, but a solution was found by carrying up the walls into miniature gables, in which these were inserted (54, 55). Dormer-gables of this sort were treated in exactly the same manner as the end gables of the houses, that is to say, finished with carved finials, copings, decorative kneelers or stone-slate verges, according to the resources at the masons' disposal. Much variety could be obtained in the design of these features, while often, particularly in Northamptonshire, a square or diamond-shaped panel would be cut in the gable-head containing a date or initials. The later type of roof-dormer, the sides of which were sometimes built up of wattle-and-daub, was a cheaper and less satisfactory expedient which tended to spoil the dignified lines of the roof.

This, throughout the uplands at least, was preponderantly of the local stone-slates, though a thatch was often substituted in lower and outlying districts. "There is no more beautiful and suitable material than these slates," wrote Sir Guy Dawber,[*] "which harmonise so admirably and seem almost to grow from the walls supporting them. When old and covered with lichens their colour is indescribably exquisite. . . . Even when new they are pleasing, as the slates are of all shades of greys, browns and yellows." It is at least a tribute to their weathering properties that innumerable old roofs in this district were ruthlessly torn down for the export prices fetched by the seasoned slates during the American building boom of the 'twenties. Perfectly in keeping, too, was the massive simplicity of the stone chimney-stacks, unrelieved except for an occasional crisp-cut course or molding (54). Square or rectangular on plan, the stacks were placed either centrally on the roof-ridge (58) or at the apex of an end gable (54, 55), and formed one of the most satisfying features of the houses.

Windows, too, played an important part in the general scheme. The lights, which were filled with lead-latticed panes and wrought-iron casements, were separated by molded mullions, and their number almost invariably diminished in each storey. Thus, in a cottage of three storeys, the ground-floor window might be of four or six lights (perhaps with

* Old Cottages and Farmhouses in the Cotswold District.

56 TYPICAL NORTHAMPTONSHIRE STONE AND THATCH: Rockingham

57 THE VILLAGE STREET, STANTON, GLOUCESTERSHIRE

58 A COTTAGE ROW AT BROADWAY, WORCESTERSHIRE

a more pronounced central mullion), the first-floor window of three, and the gable-dormer of two. The openings were treated in a uniform manner, being some 12 to 16 inches wide between the mullions, and 2 to 3 feet high. Over the heads, and returning at either side, they frequently carried the continuous drip-molding which is one of the hallmarks of the Cotswold style (55). In later houses, four-centred window-heads were sometimes used, while later still, with the spread of Renaissance detail towards the end of the seventeenth century, the windows became much wider and higher, still often retaining their mullions beneath a classic architrave, until finally both mullions and casements were superseded by sashed frames.

COTTAGE WINDOW OF COTSWOLD TYPE, SPRATTON, NORTHAMPTONSHIRE

Drawn by Sydney R. Jones.

Bay windows were used only to a minor extent in cottages. Occasionally they are to be found, of flat projection, flanking a street door and perhaps rising to dormer-gables ; or a single ground-floor bay may be combined in one composition with the door under the same stone-slated hood (58, 60). Both these arrangements, however, were more applicable to the village street than to the detached cottage. Doorways, like windows, were often surmounted by the favourite drip-molding (*p.* 60), with returns and occasionally decoratively treated kneelers. In richer examples, the heads were sometimes in the form of four-centred arches cut out of a single stone, but for humbler buildings the stone lintel predominated, occasionally sheltered by a plain projection, for which, as the Renaissance advanced, a classically treated hood might be substituted. Porches were almost unknown for cottages, and the rough types seen to-day are for the most part later additions.

In recapitulating the range of detail found in Cotswold cottages, one is apt, perhaps, to concentrate on the finer house at the expense of its poorer brother. Side by side with little masterpieces of stone construction were always dwellings of a more modest sort, walled with random rubble and often roofed with thatch (59). These, though absolutely plain in their features, and even incorporating timber window-frames and door-heads in place of stone, still for the most part unquestionably bear the Cotswold stamp. Cottages of both categories are to be found in Dorset, North - west Wiltshire, Somerset, Gloucestershire, Oxfordshire, Leicestershire, Northamptonshire, Rutland and Lincolnshire, wherever these counties are traversed or bordered by the Limestone Belt. Dorset, for instance, can show in-numerable limestone cottages of the smaller type described; the hipped roofs are covered with a thick low thatch which is often scalloped around diminutive dormers or carried in a steep catslide over a rough out-shut, though grey stone-slates of remarkably large size also make their appearance in the Purbeck district. While the majority of these cottages are of a rather severe utilitarian type, dating from the seventeenth century onwards, a few retain traces of a richer treatment in the molded mullions or dripstones of Tudor times, though these are more common in the fine farmhouses of the county, that merge almost imperceptibly into manors, with their vast and splendid barns. On the Wiltshire-Somerset border is a lovely group of villages of richer Cotswold type, such as Mells, Steeple Ashton, Lacock and Castle Combe. But the heart of Cotswold lies in the villages and townlets that cluster in the wold valleys of Gloucestershire and Oxfordshire, whose names are bywords to all lovers of the countryside. Family groups such as the Barringtons, the Swells, the Slaughters and the Rissingtons include many little houses which are the quintessence of the Cotswold style, as effective in their detail as they are happy in their surroundings and combinations. Beyond Edge Hill, where the limestone waves continue at a lower level in the "dumpling hills" of Northamptonshire, the walls of the pleasant thatched villages, such as Gretton and Moreton

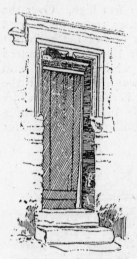

COTTAGE DOORWAY OF
COTSWOLD TYPE, MARS-
TON MAGNA, SOMERSET
Drawn by Sydney R. Jones.

59 A COTTAGE OF THE WILTSHIRE LIMESTONE: Stockton

60 A COMBINED DOORHEAD AND BAY AT CHIPPING
CAMPDEN, GLOUCESTERSHIRE

61 COLOURWASH AND PANTILES: Levisham, North Riding
of Yorkshire

62 A TRADITIONAL LAKELAND COTTAGE: Myln Beck Stock,
Westmorland

Pinkney, are sometimes interspersed with layers of reddish ironstone from the quarries around Duston and Blisworth. Rutland contains more excellent thatched villages of Cotswold type, such as Great Casterton and Exton (91, 92), and occasionally the influence strays across the county border to make its appearance in a Leicestershire farmhouse or cottage. Finally, the limestone tapers to a point along the Lincoln ridge, where stone cottages and walls continue in a narrow belt almost to the cathedral city.

From a cottage point of view, the great stone building zone of Northern England can seldom compete in charm and finish with this pure limestone country. The majority of the cottages are built either of millstone grit from the Pennines or of red sandstone (occasionally of a combination of the two); and their main attraction lies in the way their low severe lines accord with the northern background (61). In more primitive districts, such as the Border moors and the Lakeland hills, the older and rougher cottages, built with great dexterity of dry rag-masonry and roofed at a low pitch with stone-slates, are generally whitewashed over, and are seldom of more than one storey (62). The squat chimneys end in short stacks, often rounded and built of smaller stones; and in Cumberland and Westmorland there was much use of the local green stone-slate, now popular once again for suburban roofing. In the larger cottages and small-holdings of this district, a little spinning-gallery was

MULLIONED BAY-WINDOW OF COTSWOLD TYPE, BURFORD, OXFORDSHIRE

Drawn by Sydney R. Jones.

often recessed under the roof, with a wooden balustrade, where the materials were woven for the dalesmen's garments.

If the average northern cottage lacks this rough picturesqueness, it often achieves character by a kind of beetle-browed

K

sturdiness, mainly the result of using stones exceptionally large for the size of the building in masonry of the "rough ashlar" type already described (65). In addition, the window-frames and sashes are frequently painted a bright brown, with the result that they stand out at a distance against the drab background of the moors rather like eyes in a face. Where only limestone or millstone rubble were locally available, the walls, especially in East Yorkshire, were often finished with dressed quoins, door-heads and window-dressings of the sandstone that was never far away. Thatch was a common roof-covering during the eighteenth century, but has since been largely replaced by stone-slates, or, as you move south and east, rose-coloured pantiles. Pantiles are the almost exclusive covering for the cliff villages of the Yorkshire coast, such as Staithes and Robin Hood's Bay, and hold the field in the older Lincolnshire cottages, other than those of Cotswold type, whose thick walls are often colour-washed in light tints. Here, however, as throughout much of the Midlands, brick largely superseded other materials during the eighteenth century, as opposed to the more northerly counties, where the stone tradition remained little impaired, and had to its credit such charming "model village" groups as those at Cambo (Northumberland), Lowther (Westmorland) (142) and Harewood (Yorkshire). Industrialisation has wiped out many of the old Lancashire cottages, but in the unspoilt Pennine districts of the county they share the characteristics of their Yorkshire neighbours, while along the coastal fringe of the Fylde are to be seen pleasant whitewashed examples of the type shown on fig. 64. Efforts are also being made to preserve the sturdy stone cottages of the Peak District and other parts of Derbyshire, with their heavy stone-slate roofs (63), now threatened by the encroachments of motor roads, petrol pumps and tourists.

For the rest of England, the stone cottage, though it makes an occasional appearance either singly or in groups, tends to be the exception rather than the rule. The plain sandstone examples with tiled roofs which are to be seen here and there among the wood-and-wattle of the Western Midlands are of little interest, while throughout all the South-east there is only one small district, that around Horsham, Pulborough and Haslemere, that has anything approaching a village architecture in stone. This, at least as regards the farmhouses, preserves quite a Tudor tradition in the use of the yellowish local product, often with mullioned windows surmounted by

63   RUBBLE WALLS AND STONE-SLATES IN THE PEAK DISTRICT : Sparrowpit, Derbyshire

64 A COTTAGE OF THE FYLDE DISTRICT, WEETON, LANCASHIRE

65 ROUGH ASHLAR AND PANTILES AT SANDSEND, NORTH
RIDING OF YORKSHIRE

66 A DOMESTIC STRONGHOLD AT ALTARNUN, CORNWALL

67 PLASTERED STONE AT CROYDE, DEVON

68 STONE, BRICK AND THATCH AT STEDHAM, SUSSEX

drip-moldings, and occasionally with quoins and dressings of brick in place of stone. The practice known as "garetting," which consisted in inserting chips of ironstone in the mortar of the broad irregular joints, had some vogue hereabouts, and gave a distinctive texture to the masonry, while the local stone-slates formed an irregular but pleasant roof-covering in a district that has now largely "gone over" to tiles. Here the stone could not easily be worked into the thin slabs suitable for chimney-stacks, with the result that these were often built up of brick. To-day, this interesting local style survives only in a few farmhouses, but a simple type of thatched cottage also exists that is shown on fig. 68. The Isle of Wight, that little epitome of our southern geological system, can occasionally, too, show cottages of large random masonry, often combined with brick dressings and a deep thatch.

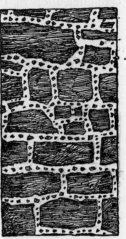

"GALLETING" OR "GARETTING" IN RUBBLE MASONRY

In the far South-west, the rugged granite houses of Cornwall and Dartmoor have often been covered with so many successive coats of whitewash that it is sometimes difficult to differentiate them from their cob neighbours, with which they are almost identical in outline, in the thatch covering that now often takes the place of stone-slates, and in the tall tapering chimneys so typical of the district, generally with a circular bake-oven outbuilt from the base of the stack. East Somerset has some villages built of a roughly dressed and rather dull-white stone, roofed with pantiles, such as Langport, Charlton Mackrell and Keinton Mandeville; but they are really not very attractive. Throughout Wiltshire and parts of Berkshire, Hampshire and Dorset are also to be found cottages built of what is known as "pudding-stone," i.e., the rough surface stone of the district collected at random. This is masonry in one of its least pretentious forms, but here again successive coats of whitewash and a thatch covering often make it difficult to distinguish the walls from cob.

There remains flint, a remarkably hard and durable building material much used in certain districts where no other stone was available, most notably Norfolk and the chalk parts of

Dorset and Hampshire. Flints could either be used for rubble masonry, or could be split and faced, often with " garetted " joints in which the chips and splinters were inserted, as much to strengthen the mortar as for decorative effect. Quoins and dressings were either of stone or brick, and in more ambitious buildings the flint was often chequered or diapered with these materials with rich and pleasant effect, though this treatment is hardly found in cottages except, perhaps, on the Dorset-Wiltshire border and in parts of East Anglia and Kent, where the texture of the walls is sometimes a remarkable conglomeration of flint, pudding-stone and brick. In Wilt-shire walls knapped flints are often made into a rough chequer pattern with blades of stone or chalk, while in Hampshire layers of flint are set in brickwork, even, with neat effect, in the small panels of half-timber filling. Figs. 71, 72 show typical Wiltshire examples of this treatment, while fig. 70 shows a Norfolk use of unsplit flint cobbles for rubble walling, such as is to be found in many seaboard districts. Figs. 73, 74 provide, per-haps, the best idea of the scope of the material for smaller domestic purposes,

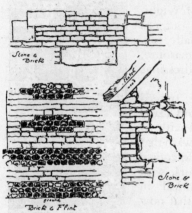

VARIETIES OF STONE, BRICK AND FLINT WALLING FROM HAMPSHIRE AND DORSET

Drawn by Sydney R. Jones.

showing how delicately it can be combined with brick quoins, arched window-heads and chimneys, and how well suited is the typical Norfolk covering of red pantiles. In seaboard East Anglia there is an occasional use of rough pebbles set to a fairly smooth surface for walling instead of the rounded " kidney " flints, or in other parts, of larger rounded stones too intractable to be squared. In both Norfolk and Suffolk flint cottages are occasionally colour-washed, or the side walls covered with a thick coating of tar—an effect which is by no means disagreeable.

70 KIDNEY-FLINTS AND PANTILES AT
BLAKENEY, NORFOLK

69 DRY MASONRY AT GRASMERE,
WESTMORLAND

71, 72 WILTSHIRE CONGLOMERATES: Flint, Brick and Pudding Stone at Great Durnford

73 BRICK AND COURSED FLINT AT BLAKENEY, NORFOLK

74 RUBBLE-FLINT AND BRICK AT BAYLHAM, SUFFOLK

75 STONE-SLATE ROOFING IN THE COTSWOLDS: Arlington Row,
Bibury, Gloucestershire

VII

ROOFING AND WEATHERPROOFING

I. Roofing

The methods of roof-covering in use at the present day comprise thatch, slates of split stone or geological slate, and tiles, whether burnt, flat or pantiles—or of the recent asbestos variety. One form of medieval roofing, shingles of split wood, has gone entirely out of domestic use, though it is still employed in a plain fashion on church spires in stoneless districts, and is of common occurrence in Colonial America on house roofs. To take a distant comparison, a form of small wooden shingle is used effectively in the Duchy of Luxembourg, and one example near Vianden duplicates almost exactly the decorative tile-patterning on a cottage in Surrey recorded by Mr Curtis Green.

Stone-slates.—Of these roof-coverings, thatch and stone-slates date from early days, tiles mostly from the seventeenth century onwards, blue or green slates (used generally) from the nineteenth, and asbestos tiles from the twentieth ; the last two are mostly employed on new buildings and are as convenient and cheap as they are æsthetically objectionable. Let us first consider Stone-slates, which are of local occurrence in the North, especially in Derbyshire, West Yorkshire ; in the Limestone Belt, particularly in the Cotswolds and their extension to Northamptonshire and Rutland, and as an outlier in the Horsham district and elsewhere in Sussex. The Romans roofed their buildings in Britain extensively with stone-slates secured with iron nails, which were not used again until centuries later. The famous quarries at Stonesfield, Oxfordshire, produced three sizes of slates during the Middle Ages ; and the well-known stone-slates of the Cotswolds originated there, or from the equally celebrated quarries at Colly Weston in Northamptonshire. There are, or were, a number of local stone-slates not widely known outside their own particular district ; it is not very easy to obtain records of them. A case in point is the dark Smithland stone-slates from Charnwood Forest in Leicestershire, named locally " Smidland Slabs," which were utilised for roofing and other purposes from pre-Conquest days to about fifty years ago, when the popularity of red tiles caused the workings to be closed. The slates are nearly half an inch in thickness, and quite imperishable ; they are still stripped from old cottages to roof modern buildings.

Slates proper were used locally before the Industrial Revolution in Wales and the Lake District; before the days of large-scale mechanical production they were smaller, thicker and more irregular than the modern variety, and formed a quite effective and appropriate roofing. It is not inevitable that slate roofing should be harsh in texture and monotonous in effect. In the Duchy of Luxembourg there is frequent use of a thin variety of slate, half-rounded at the lower end, which is laid in diagonal rows with an agreeably diversified result. But the machine-regular splitting of Welsh blue slates commenced fairly early in the nineteenth century, and their use has spread universally with the quick convenience of railway transport. Hence the indigenous stone-slates went entirely out of use for a time, and ceased to be made, although they would be preserved from demolished buildings and used for re-roofing or new houses. Their manufacture has now been revived, but it must be regretfully admitted that however admirable in itself, their use is economically anachronistic. The digging of the Stonesfield slates, through underground tunnels, involves an amount of hard physical labour distasteful to the younger generation to-day.

The laying of the stone-slates called for the practice of skilled craftsmanship; they diminished in size towards the ridge, and were cleverly worked round valleys, avoiding the use of lead or tiles frequent in the case of thatch. The late Sir Guy Dawber has described the method of roofing with them in his *Cotswold Cottages*, and has pointed out that they required stronger roof timbers and more care in fixing; but a well-made stone roof is, with slight repair, almost imperishable. He gives a list of the slaters' names for the different varieties of individual slates used in the Cotswolds, names which he says the workmen are shy of using before strangers; among them may be mentioned the Cussome, Wivetts, Bachelors, Movedays, Cuttings, and Cocks, long and short. The invaluable Randle Holme, writing from Chester in his *Academy of Armour* in 1688, gives a list of contemporary slate names of an almost unbelievable picturesqueness. Among them we cannot forbear to mention Haghattees, long and short, Farwells, Chilts, Warnetts, Batchlers, Wivetts, Rogue-why-Winkest-thou, and Jenny-why-Gettest-thou. On the other hand, the heavier varieties of the North and Horsham need a roof of less pitch, and if not well laid they will drag on the pegs, and need to be cemented over at the joints to keep the structure watertight.

76 THE WIDE SWEEP OF STONE-SLATED ROOF AT
ARLINGTON ROW, BIBURY, GLOUCESTERSHIRE

77 SLATERS AT WORK IN THE COTSWOLDS

78　A COTTAGE ROW AT THORNTON-LE-DALE, YORKSHIRE, STONE-BUILT AND PANTILED

The effect of old stone-slate roofs is always harmonious and pleasing—to take a humble instance, the little square two-storey buildings which dot the fields in Swaledale in the West Yorkshire moorlands seem to grow out of the hills themselves, so that it might be said that the actual haystacks are of stone. The old slates are dappled or encrusted with a thick growth of moss, lichens and houseleek, and form an equally appropriate finish to the austere cottages of the North, the half-timbered buildings of the South-eastern counties or the houses built of large blocks of the fire- or rag-stones of the same area. There is a subtle, wavy irregularity when they are fixed on hand-riven timber; in comparison, the effect of blue Welsh slates, thin and skinny, set on exactly cut rafters, even though cheaper and quick to construct, cannot be anything but hard, bleak and unsympathetic. The same remarks apply to the use of corrugated iron instead of stone-slates for barns and other farm-buildings: when a farmer at Middle Littleton, Worcestershire, tells that one of the building protection societies paid him £1,000 to continue the stone roofing of his splendid barn and avoid the use of tinned metal corrugations, it can be realised how heavily the economic scales are weighted against the older materials and methods.

TILES.—It is somewhat surprising to find that the usual plain burnt roofing tiles are not only rather late in the field as regards introduction, but are also mostly limited to the South-east and Midland areas in regard to their occurrence. The convenient and useful tile is very prevalent for domestic roof-coverings of the present day, for the hard blue Welsh slates have been chiefly relegated since Victorian days to the lower grades of urban house property. But for old cottages tiles are to be found in regular use in Kent, Surrey and Sussex, where they first displaced thatch quite a long time ago; here also they are found side by side with thatch and Horsham stone-slates. They also occur in the districts of the Midlands and Welsh Border, away from the Limestone Belt with its Colly Weston and Stonesfield slates; here again they hold the field in dispute with thatch and stone-slates, as also in southern East Anglia, where they are found on plastered village rows (137) and isolated houses. It is a remarkable fact that the common tile, apart from the pantile, is not often found as a covering for stone-built cottages, which favour stone-slates or thatch; but with the austere stone cottages of Shropshire are found tile roofings, possibly due to the proximity of the Broseley factory by the Severn.

There is no doubt that the Roman form of tile was the pantile, which must have given a somewhat southern aspect to the Roman buildings in England. In old writings the tiler is called *tegulator*, and was obviously an important person among the building craftsmen of the community. Bricks, of course, were thin in shape and were frequently called *tigel*, or tile, so that it is not easy to differentiate in early accounts between bricks for the wall and tiles for the roof.

Regulations as early as the thirteenth century had ordered that thack, or thatch, in large towns should be proscribed in favour of tiling, but on account of the fuel needed tiles were, until the end of the sixteenth or the early part of the seventeenth century, decidedly scarce and precious. In one of the Paston letters, the request occurs : " Master Stoby begs loan or alms of tylle to roof one of his fayrest chambers which standyth half-uncovered for default of tylle " ; and another letter, dated 1475, announces, referring to tiles, that " there is none to get for no money." Frequently, when mulcting deliquents for disobeying regulations or petty laws, the fine was ordered to be paid in a number of tiles. Instances are found in the later Middle Ages at Reading, when, for an act of disobedience to the Mayor, John Bristow was ordered to pay 4000 tiles, while if a barber kept his shop open later than ten o'clock in the evening, he had to pay a fine of 300 tiles to the Town Hall. It is curious to find that some of the absurd and vexatious regulations in regard to shop-opening, from a fresh crop of which we are now suffering, were actively in force nearly five hundred years ago. In some houses in Devonshire at about the close of the Middle Ages, the first ridge tile at the gable-end represented a horse and rider ; it is possible that a few of these still survive.

Tiles were also employed extensively and in considerable variety for wall-hanging in the South-eastern counties, so far west as Berkshire ; this method is referred to under *Weatherproofing* (*p.* 77). Mr. Curtis Green, R.A., in his account of *Surrey Cottages* mentions the practice of dabbing an occasional tile with a stiff brush to produce a rougher surface, which gave a different effect when weathered by allowing the readier growth of moss and lichens.

The asbestos tile is a post-war product and need only be mentioned briefly here ; it is usually referred to slangily as " pink," but is in reality of a raw red which, so far as can be seen, does not tone or mellow with the effect of time. Fortunately, asbestos roofs are confined so far to the disfigurement of new villas, bungalows and council housing-schemes, and are rarely if ever added to old cottages. But the proximity of a few asbestos-tiled buildings will cause strident dissonance with a group of old cottages, with which they will remain permanently out of harmony. Mr. Arthur Stratton, F.R.I.B.A., has striven to get builders and owners in his Sussex district to adopt a quieter tone of brown, or other more reposeful shades, in which this variety of tile is obtainable, though the fact does not seem very generally known or applied.

PANTILES are of comparatively recent introduction, and began to be made in England about the middle of the eighteenth century, after they had long been imported from the Continent, principally from the Netherlands. There are a number of varieties in shape and colour, and apart from purely modern buildings they are to be found in several well-marked but isolated districts, chief among which are the flatter districts of Yorkshire, especially on the eastern side of the Vale of York—though stone-slates are the standard roofing method in the moorland clefts of the western dales—Norfolk, Suffolk and East Anglia generally, and the eastern part of Somerset around Langport. In the East Anglian counties they blend excellently with the cottages of mixed flint or brick. The fine group of Exmoor-type cottages at the famous Packhorse Bridge at Allerford near Porlock is now roofed with pantiles, but its original covering was thatch, as is illustrated in Oliver's *Old Cottages* from an older photograph : this change is typical of what has taken place in North Yorkshire and other districts during the nineteenth century. In East Anglia an almost black, dull-finished or slightly glazed pantile is now in fairly frequent use, and gives a parti-coloured effect when used patchwork-like with the regular bright red type.

With THATCHING we come to the interesting survival in a developed form of the most primitive form of roof-covering. There is little doubt that the first attempts at dwellings in this country, such as the Neolithic hut-circles, were roofed with turves, or branches of heather, or reeds over brushwood spread between the poles. That thatch has been able to maintain itself as a practicable means of covering for mixed types of human dwellings for some 10,000 years proves that it is not only picturesque, but eminently efficacious and satisfactory. It is pleasant to think of the group of Devon cottages tucked round a great barton in a deep, winding combe, the rounded roof-outlines of a Wiltshire Downland hamlet, the high-peaked black-thatched gables of colour-washed Suffolk villages, and even the occasional thatch survival of the Yorkshire Vales. And still the low-browed casements of Cornish fisher cottages look under eaves of shaggy thatch across the Atlantic coves, and the same type of roofing gives snug protection from the winds of the Northumbrian Fells. As Mr. Blair Imrie has well put it :—*

There is no other roof which almost at once becomes an integral part of the countryside. It is the only roof-covering which is as much at home in the Derbyshire dales as in the Fen District, and it is as happy with the cob and granite walls of Devonshire as it is with Sussex half-timber and flint. A thatched roof has a wonderful suavity of line, and its colour and texture are delightful. Even the crudity of new red bricks is softened when crowned with thatch, and many a poorly-designed building would be redeemed by a covering of reeds or straw. There is, too, no better roof to live under. From a test made by the writer it was found that a reed-thatched house was about 10 per cent. cooler in summer than a tiled house adjoining, and it is no doubt correspondingly warmer in winter.

It is frequently stated in books that thatch is fast dying out, largely through lack of the craftsmen to carry on the work. This is nonsensical pessimism ; there have to be thatchers enough to keep in repair the thousands of thatched cottages. In a recent Building Trades Directory there are some 175 names of thatchers, mostly concentrated in the Southern Midlands, East Anglia and the South-west. They include such pleasant-sounding names as Ashplant, Habgood, Hurry, Retter and Quantock, the latter appropriately enough in two parts of Somerset. Anyone who goes about the countryside will see, apart from ricks and haystacks, plenty of thatched cottages repaired or re-roofed, and may even catch the craftsman at his work (79-81).

Thatch is also used for new country houses of a superior type, and a well-known road-house on one of the arterial roads outside London is covered entirely with it—a splendid example of craftsmanship, a *tour de force* indeed, by a firm of thatchers from North Walsham, Norfolk.

This type of roofing has, however, had to maintain itself against two serious drawbacks, firstly, the discouragement offered by that particularly exacting form of bureaucratic control which has taken in hand English building since the middle of the nineteenth century, and which, from an

---

* " The Case for Thatching," *Country Life*, Dec. 4th, 1920.

79 THATCHING IN DORSET

80, 81　THATCHERS AT WORK

exaggerated fear of the danger of fire, brought into the open countryside the regulations only excusable in a close-packed urban area.   Hence there were formulated regulations antagonistic to thatch and half-timber construction, two of the most effective and characteristic forms of English vernacular building.   This rigidity is now fortunately relaxed, but only in part.

The other drawback with which thatch has had to contend is nineteenth-century snobbishness—as the more primitive form of roofing it was held to be humble and inferior.   This sentiment goes back a long way further than that arcadia of snobbery, the 1800's, for Palsgrave is quoted in 1530 as giving as an indication of his poverty that his house is thatched instead of tiled.   Many East Anglian churches were thatched, of which a fair number still survive, especially in Norfolk, but many incumbents in the period of Victorian " restoration " congratulated themselves on replacing what in their narrow-mindedness they considered an inferior and unsuitable roofing. An amusing instance was seen in Reydon Church, Suffolk, about 1880, when the side of the roof next to the road was slated, but the other, more away from public view, was thatched; both are now roofed miserably with slates.   The late Dr. Cox used to interest himself in recording lists of the number of thatched churches remaining.

The northern version " thack " is used generally for any form of roofing, and " Stonethack " is a surname of occasional occurrence.   There are scanty but extremely interesting medi-eval records of thatch, and we must mention a valuable account of practical methods by Harry Best, published by the Surtees Society as *Rural Economy in Yorkshire in 1641*. A number of accounts of thatching practice have been written, though the urbanisation of England has rendered the craft a mysterious one to many observers of the country.   Among these notes are series in Jefferies' *Wild Life in a Southern County*, and in Sir H. Rider Haggard's *A Farmer's Year*; all are of interest, but none completely covers the ground; and even Innocent's invaluable chapter needs supplementing.   A full historic, practical and regional account of thatching has still to be written, and a series of record films taken; only the briefest outline is possible here.   We can at least rejoice that in thatching we have the one building craft which has defied mechanised standardisation—it is not only highly traditional but highly individual, and much depends not only on regional methods but also on the craftsman's individual working out, and the use of tools which he may have himself improvised or adapted ; a few of these will be named later on.

The materials used in thatching are the straw of the cultivated grasses, wheat, oats or rye, preferably (but rarely) reaped by the sickle, as machine-reaping damages the fibres, which also suffer from the attentions of the threshing-machine. Uncultivated grasses are also used in East Anglia, especially reeds, which form the finest material and will afford durability for anything up to a hundred years. In Wiltshire a particularly strong kind of straw was rather confusingly termed " reed," and in North Wales and the Scottish Border rushes are also utilised. In addition ling is occasionally employed, and turves or sods may form the groundwork. There are other materials of quite local use.

The actual methods of applying the thatch are divided by Innocent into four types : sewing on the thatch to the rafters ; pinning it down by a system of rods and broaches, *i.e.* hairpin-like pointed sticks ; working the material into a foundation of turves ; and securing the roofing by a series of weighted ropes passed over it. These methods may be used in various forms of combination, and the result is a remarkable variety of processes. Nevertheless, the second is by far the most usual way of working in England, though the first is also found fairly commonly, and the two are sometimes used together effectively and advantageously. The third method of combining the thatch with turves is an unusual and possibly rather crude one, which only occurs in the North and in Scotland, while the fourth, rope-thatching, the most primitive, is confined entirely to the Celtic fringe ; it is not the regular practice in Wales, at all events for domestic buildings, but is found in the Isle of Man (82), Cornwall, the Western Highlands (83) and in Ireland, especially on the Atlantic seaboard. By this method the thatch, which is heaped into something of a dome-shape, is criss-crossed with ropes of straw or ordinary material to prevent its being blown off bodily by the gales. The ropes are either weighted by being lashed at their ends to rocks, which are occasionally as big as young boulders (83), or more systematically, are secured as in the Isle of Man, to projecting pieces of slate (82), or as in Donegal, to pegs provided in the walls. Thatch is occasionally held down by old fishing-nets. The roof-covering is occasionally treated with a coat of whitewash, and often forms the soil for a varied crop of grasses, houseleek, etc. The latter is said on occasion to

82 A FISHERMAN'S COTTAGE IN THE ISLE OF MAN: plaster
over rough boulders, and a primitive thatch

83 A PRIMITIVE SHIELING AT SKEBOST BRIDGE, ISLE OF SKYE.
Note the rough thatch enclosing the chimney and weighted down by stones

85 BAYLHAM, SUFFOLK

84 KERSEY, SUFFOLK

have been purposely planted in Ireland in criss-cross rows with variegated effect.

There is no occasion nor space here for a detailed account of thatching, the preparation of its materials, and their weaving into finished roofing. The subject is of exceptional interest and would form an excellent thesis for an R.I.B.A. Diploma ; it would certainly test the powers of an able investigator-student, for the actual process is very difficult to express clearly in words by or to a layman, and many accounts fail to convey it intelligibly. Methods of course differ in detail remarkably, both locally and individually, and with the use of straw, reeds or other materials, while the nomenclature is highly technical and again varies with each district in the most puzzling way. Several pages of an English Dialect Dictionary could be easily devoted to thatching terms and their areas.

The thatcher has various ways of preparing his straw, removing short and broken pieces and getting it level and parallel ; this is called " yelming " in the West. This may in the South-west even be effected by a power-driven machine attached to an ordinary steam-engine. Then in Dorset the " reed-drawing," as it is called, is sometimes carried out in a press made of a bench and an adjustable beam. The straw may also be combed. In addition, the thatcher has prepared his bundles of rods, or " ledgers," and " broaches," or " spars " or " spicks," the latter split wands of willow or hazel, pointed at both ends, with a single twist in the middle for ricks and a double twist for house work ; the skilled fabrication of these is described by Richard Jefferies and Sir H. Rider Haggard, and in detail by Mr. Hennell in *Change on the Farm*. The thatcher's very varied, and often individual, equipment may include two knee-pads for prolonged standing on his ladder, a " fork," Y-shaped, and variously termed, for carrying the " yelms " or bundles up to the roof, secured when full by a piece of string across the top ; his little sharp bill-hook for cutting the spars, a small mallet for beating the straw, a pair of shears for trimming, and a ligget, or leggatt, having a long diagonally-set handle and a square face, either with wooden ridges or old horse-nails beaten flat, for knocking or smoothing straw or reed into position (81).

Possibly two women assistants have been busy " yelming " and wetting the straw, which the thatcher spreads on the roof, sometimes securing it temporarily with a setting needle.

M

The craftsman works from the eaves upwards and from left to right. The material is spread out, raked or combed to a smooth surface, downward in the case of straw, upward for reeds. Next, assuming that sewing is adopted as the securing method, for the layers next the rafters at least, the thatcher takes tar-rope in his foot-long steel needle and passes it through to his assistant in the building, underneath the rafters. The rope is twined round the horizontal laths laid across the rafters, which are much more widely spaced than for a tiled roof; occasionally the twine is tied at the intersection of laths and rafters. Reed-plait may be used in Cambridgeshire instead of laths, but the old English foundation was wattle. Then the eaves are trimmed with the shears, and the work is ready for the next bundle. Usually the layers above the first are pinned to those below by rows of the rods or "ledgers," which are sometimes thrust into the straw and tied to the rafters at the other end; they are usually covered by the topmost layer, but can be seen when the roof is under repair; sometimes across older roofs the long threadlike lines of rods can be traced like stitches in a piece of needlework (24, 88). Crabbe called this, as a sign of lamentable dilapidation, "vile bands of the thatch," and on an old East Anglian roof the effect is certainly untidy, reminiscent of too visible hairpins on a dishevelled head of hair (87). Again, when working on an old underlying thatch or on upper layers when the rafters cannot be reached, the rods are pinned down by the hazel or willow "broaches" or "spars"; with their hairpin shape they give the same tightness as the pins in a woman's long tresses. Straw can be bent over at the roof-ridge, but the tougher reed needs a cap or shell of sedge over the top for weatherproofing, as appears in some of the East Anglian cottages illustrated (89); this is held in place by rows of rods with varied crisscrossing between. If the topmost material of this cap has somehow got displaced, the close-set broaches stick out like a forest of nails. The cap ends in a series of sharply projecting V-shaped tongues, a patterning often repeated lower down on the roof, with sometimes a third division of semicircular scallops, as at South Cove (89). In any case, the last coat of thatch is thus pinned at the roof-ridge and eaves with one or more lines of rods; when the smaller rods, named slats, are arranged diamond-wise between two rows, it is called, "dimenting," and makes a pleasant decorative finish. It is, however, a little disconcerting to see the demands of com-

86 THE ROUGH ASHLAR AND PLAIN THATCH OF OXFORDSHIRE IN A WROXTON
COTTAGE ROW

87 NEAR HATFIELD, HERTFORDSHIRE (now demolished)

88 FYFIELD, ESSEX

OLD THATCH WORN TO SHOW THE "RODS" ON
WEATHERBOARDED COTTAGES

89 EAST ANGLIAN THATCHING *IN EXCELSIS*, AT
SOUTH COVE, SUFFOLK

90 A NEAT ROOFING OF PANTILES ADDS CHARM TO THIS OTHER-
WISE RATHER FEATURELESS BRICK COTTAGE AT STRADSETT,
NORFOLK

91, 92 TYPICAL THATCHED COTTAGES OF THE EASTERN
LIMESTONE BELT, AT EXTON, RUTLAND

mercial enterprise met by the word "ICES" outlined in rods, as in a recent case. Some cottages in Suffolk and the South (42) have an extra layer curved around the gable-end, with visible rods.

If much has been written in scattered and sporadic fashion about thatchers' methods, it is essential that some thatch-lover should do what has not yet been attempted, *i.e.* work out a careful comparative account of the various local types of thatching—how, for instance, the East Anglian style differs from the thatch of the South-west, how the gable-ends and

A "TOUR DE FORCE" OF THATCHING, BEAULIEU, HAMPSHIRE
Drawn by Sydney R. Jones.

roof-ridges are treated, how the roofing is brought over and round the dormers, how hips and valleys are handled, etc. Little can be done here to define these local distinctions; for example, the eastern roofs are of steeper pitch, and the thatch is cocked up with perky sharpness over the dormers. The South-western thatch has a peculiar velvet texture, loves wavy lines and wanders around corners. About Ampthill (South Bedfordshire) the dormer thatch is cut with particular sharpness into an almost complete semicircle. Wiltshire cottages have their own dormer thatch-shapes, and often each porch of a row will have its little hat of thatch. The mud or cob walls have also their own little roofs of thatch in

Wiltshire and the adjacent counties. It has recently been observed that in East Yorkshire a layer of pantiles has actually been applied over the underlying thatch.

The danger from fire has been very largely exaggerated,—the question has been gone into very thoroughly by Mr. Blair Imrie, in his paper already quoted. Pressure should be brought to bear upon insurance companies to reduce any disproportionately high premiums, a result of that tendency to be scared by imaginary bogies which is one of their most salient characteristics. Agitation should be directed, too, against any vague and woolly attitude of controlling authorities, which should get the local bodies into line and bring pressure to bear upon those who cling to the obsolete narrowness of the Victorian " Model " Bye-laws. All who love English tradition should see that this beautiful, cheap and suitable method of roofing comes into its own again.

The huge hooks used to tear the burning thatch from the roof may be seen preserved at Thaxted Guildhall, Essex, the churches of Yaxley, Huntingdonshire and Eaton Bray, Bedfordshire, while in Jekyll's *Old English Household Life* is illustrated a curious contraption in which the hook was mounted on a wheeled framework and trundled to the scene of the fire.

Sometimes there are minor drawbacks in the use of thatch ; Mrs. A. L. Merritt describes plaintively the painful effects of tunnelling by hordes of starlings ; these can be averted by a coat of wire-netting, though that practice is objectionable from the amount of rubbish which gets caught up in its meshes. In Suffolk, wire-netting is sometimes placed along the roof-ridge and over the eaves. There are also boyish memories of exciting earwig-hunts when going to bed in a thatched cottage in the Isle of Wight. According to the late Miss O'Neill in *Devonshire Idylls*, her old widowed Mary counted her roof, put on by her husband's hands, one of the chief of her (to us very meagre) blessings : " What can a body want more than a full belly and a warm back and a good thatchen roof over their heads ? "

Let us think of the results which the thatcher has achieved with his very ordinary materials and few simple appliances—as much a joy to contemplate as to live under, as decorative as snug, as inexpensive as durable. He has earned, and it should be our grateful privilege to accord him, a high place among the great line of English building craftsmen, and when he gets a chance to show his mettle in the delightful little

93   A DORSET COTTAGE ROW, KIMMERIDGE

94 TILEHANGING COMBINED WITH WEATHERBOARDING
AT GROOMBRIDGE, KENT

whimsical straw ornaments on stacks, and the lovely miniature cornricks for harvest festivals, who shall be churlish enough to deny him the well-merited title of an artist of the countryside?

II. WEATHERPROOFING

TILEHANGING.—Frequently in old timber houses the filling between the timbers shrank or decayed, and the house itself settled, so that it became imperative to devise some means of weatherproofing; a process carried out in the case of cottages in three ways—by tilehanging, by plastering the exterior, and by weatherboarding. These methods are in certain districts used in combination (94, 104).

To consider Tilehanging first, it is probable that the practice did not become general until well on in the seventeenth century, and during the course of the next one, when an abundant supply of the tiles was available. Up to the close of the Middle Ages, like glass, they had largely been imported. The practice, especially indigenous in Kent, Surrey and Sussex, spread to a slight extent into Hampshire, but there is a well-marked area of particularly good building craftsmanship in Berkshire where tilehanging is quite commonly found, as in the delightful villages under the Downs, such as the Hagbournes, the Hendreds, Harwell, Blewbury, Aston Tirrold and their fellows. The practice is scarcely known in the Midlands, East Anglia and the North.

The tiles used for wall-hanging were, as a rule, flatter and thinner than those on the roofs, were hung on oak laths with pins of hazel or willow, or sometimes of elder, and bedded solid in lime and hair mortar, making a satisfactory and permanently weatherproof wall. When judiciously applied the practice is entirely satisfactory, as the colour and texture are distinctly attractive. Frequently the bright red of the original tones has faded, but in the course of years they acquire beautiful grey, yellowish and green tints from lichen and stains, while occasionally tiles of purplish hue are mixed with the others, so that there is a very pleasant play of colour on the overlapping rows.

The most frequent positions for tilehanging are on the first floor, often on the gable-end and occasionally on the whole front or side of a house. But usually it is confined to the upper floor, the ground floor being of plain brick, or occasionally of stone.

The old workmen handled their tiles with that instinctive

N

sense of texture and feeling for materials which was one of their outstanding characteristics. In partially tilehung houses there may be a variety of tiles with half-timbering and brick filling (97), while on occasion in Kent and Sussex, as will be seen, the other protective methods of plastering and weather-boarding are also combined separately (148) or together on the same building. In the Berkshire district already mentioned, tiling is largely confined to the faces of gables and of the smaller gables of dormers, and occasionally the oriels under-neath them. A partially decayed house in Marlborough seemed to show that a wall could be finished with horizontal laths for tilehanging from its first construction.

There is a considerable variety of patterning. The plain rectangular tile is, of course, frequently used (95-6), and the village of Goudhurst on its sharply rising hill is remarkable for the extensive use in bright deep-red colour of this type

PRESTWICK   HASCOMBE   EWHURST WITLEY   HASLEMERE

TYPES OF SURREY TILEHANGING

Drawn by W. Curtis Green, R.A.

of tile on the walls. A half-round tile of fish-scale type is also frequently found (97), either the plain semicircle or with a straight flange at each side, in several slightly differing types. The rectangular and the round tiles are frequently used in combination in varying numbers of rows (98), and the writers venture to differ from one or two eminent authori-ties on domestic building in feeling that it is not necessary to claim that the exclusive use of plain rectangular tiles is pre-ferable to a combined use of different patterns which, if applied with the skill and feeling of the old craftsman, gives a pleasant effect of variety and a liveliness of texture. It is, however, remarkable that Victorian attempts to handle this method in the pretty-picturesque period of imitation Queen Anne have usually ended in an effect of overdone frippery, showing how, when the feeling for materials has been lost, an excellent method can be largely prostituted.

An alternative method of weatherproofing is SLATEHANGING (100), which is typically found in Cornwall, and in Devon be-

95 TILES, BRICK AND BOARDS AT BURWASH, SUSSEX

96 A TYPICAL TILE-HUNG KENTISH ROW AT GOUDHURST

97 FISHTAIL TILES ON A HALF-TIMBER COTTAGE AT WITLEY, SURREY

99   A PLAIN TILE-HUNG KENTISH COTTAGE
AT YALDING

98   VARIETY IN TILING NEAR CHIDDINGSTONE,
KENT

100 CORNISH SLATE-HANGING AT ST. IVES

tween Exeter and Plymouth, though it also occurs at Dunstar
and occasionally in Wales. Some houses of the sixteenth century
are slatehung, and the practice continued till the early nineteenth. The earlier examples show patterning by the use of
slates set straight and diagonally, and by differences in spacing,
but later whole fronts were covered from top to bottom with
rows of straight-hung slates. There is a feeling of comfortable
neatness about the wide expanses of silvery-grey or bluish
slate-walling, and a sense of local appropriateness which
would be entirely lacking were slatehanging carried out in an
alien district.

PLASTERING.—The method that will be now considered is
the complete or partial plastering of the exterior of a house,
often originally timber-framed. The method of plastering
panels, leaving the timber exposed, current on the Welsh
Border and elsewhere, is mentioned under methods of filling.

Plastering is probably of late-seventeenth or eighteenth
century date, and is as widespread and effective as the alternative methods. Naturally the cob cottages of Devonshire, and
any of a mud consistency, are also plastered, as the walls
quickly decay if the weather can gain entrance to them. But
that process is dealt with under Cob building, and we are at
present considering the contemporary or subsequent plastering
of timber-framed houses. It is, however, interesting to see
that much the same effect may be produced, for the dazzling
white plaster of a Devonshire cob finish has much in common
with the general appearance of a Suffolk village.

The chief district of plastered houses is East Anglia in
general, though there is but little in Norfolk, and that chiefly
for mud building, while in Essex weatherboarding is preferred
in the south and up to the middle of the county. Plastered
houses are of fairly frequent occurrence in Kent, and some
treated partially are found in Surrey, but the headquarters of
the process may be regarded as a large circle having its centre
at the point where Essex, Cambridgeshire and Suffolk meet.
In this connection East Anglia may be reckoned to include
the southern half of Cambridgeshire, North-east Hertfordshire,
some of South Bedfordshire and all Huntingdonshire. Many
of these plastered houses are the old timber ones covered
over, but later ones were frequently intended from the first to
be covered with plaster, and are consequently only roughly
timbered, a fact not understood by injudicious restorers who
strip away the old plaster covering to bring to light the
underlying timbers, which were never meant to be exposed.

The composition of this old plaster was of lime, sand and bullocks' hair, with the admixture of a certain proportion of fresh cow-dung, and road-scrapings which provided ground stone-grit and horse manure. Straw and stable urine were other materials which occasionally found a place. The mixture was, according to Professor Lethaby, " well-washed, beaten, stirred, and tested so carefully, and for so long a time, that, when laid, it was as tough as leather."

The plaster gives a smooth surface finish, frequently gleaming white, but broken up by the projections of the building. Many East Anglian villages or town streets consist almost entirely of plaster houses, such as Clare, Kersey, Haughley, Ickleton, Hartest, Foulmire (*alias* Fowlmere), etc., and the method reaches its highest effectiveness in the colour-washed hamlets of central or southern Suffolk, as in a group adjoining Lavenham, including Kettlebaston, Brent and Monks Eleigh. These Suffolk houses are often washed in light blues, greens and pinks. In South Huntingdonshire there is a use, with effective results, of orange or various shades of brown, as at Kimbolton and its surrounding district. All the most beautiful villages of this area are thus treated, and therefore what is perhaps the finest village cluster in England is plastered.

Though attractive and in itself pleasant, there is no doubt that this plastering largely masks the character of East Anglian timber building, except that it can be seen that the overhanging storey is common on the first floors both of gables and the long sides of houses (37). The plastering is usually plain, and pargetting is not particularly frequent on cottages, this more ambitious decorative treatment being reserved for farms and larger private houses, such as the former Sun Inn at Saffron Walden, Colneford House, Crown House, Newport, and the example by the churchyard at Clare. Occasionally, however, the plaster of an East Anglian cottage is divided into plain panels, or diversified partially or wholly by such combed or pricked patterns as scalloped circles, lined chequers or intersecting cables (*p.* 81). It is unfortunate that the tradition of this pargetting seems to be entirely lost. A floral pattern was at times found in Kent, especially in the gables, of which a few examples remain, as in a cottage near Maidstone. Two fine examples of pargetting are a remarkable house at Wivenhoe and the splendid running frieze of Bishop Bonner's cottage at East Dereham (108); it is not certain, however, if either of these was originally of cottage status. Occasionally in larger examples the late seventeenth century

102 BACK GARDEN

101 BACK YARD

103 A TYPICAL EAST ANGLIAN COTTAGE COUPLE,
BATTISFORD, SUFFOLK

104 PLASTER AND WEATHERBOARDING AT FINCHINGFIELD,
ESSEX

105 TOO PROUD FOR ITS PRIVY: Elmsett, Suffolk

106 THE HEART OF EAST ANGLIA: Cavendish, Suffolk

107 SIBTON, SUFFOLK

108 BISHOP BONNER'S COTTAGE, EAST DEREHAM, NORFOLK

EAST ANGLIAN PARGETING

plasterwork has been stripped off, showing the original timbering, as at the Guildhall, Thaxted and " Paycockes," Coggeshall.   If this is not carefully done, there is often an effect of

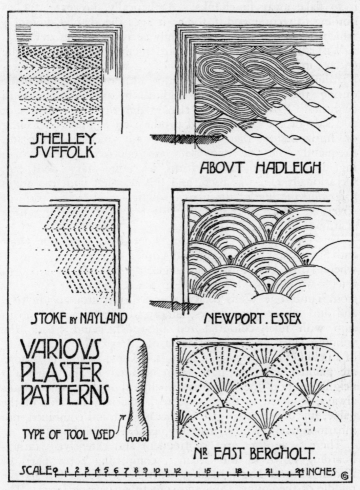

SHELLEY. SUFFOLK

ABOVT HADLEIGH

STOKE BY NAYLAND

NEWPORT. ESSEX

VARIOVS PLASTER PATTERNS

TYPE OF TOOL VSED

Nº EAST BERGHOLT.

SCALE 0 1 2 3 4 5 6 7 8 9 10 11 12   15   18   21   24 INCHES

DECORATIVE PLASTER-COMBING IN EAST ANGLIA

Drawn by Edwin Gunn.

inappropriate smartening and injudicious restoration.   It is not often, however, that anyone has bothered to strip the plaster and expose the timber of old cottages, though a fine row has recently been well treated in this way at Elham, Kent.

CEMENT-COVERING may be considered as a bastard form of

o

plastering. It was apparently prevalent during a bad period
of the nineteenth century. It is possibly efficacious in certain
cases, though there is a tendency, if not skilfully applied, for
it to flake away in chunks. Æsthetically, however, it has
nothing to recommend it, for as it ages the shabby dinginess
which is its main characteristic only becomes accentuated.

WEATHERBOARDING.—The third method of rendering the
cottage immune from the attacks of the weather is by weatherboarding, which is usually a later addition, probably made
during the course of the eighteenth or early-nineteenth
centuries. The long timber slats stretch right across the face
and side of the cottages and produce an emphasised feeling
of horizontality that is not by any means unpleasant.
Frequently one or two slats are contrived with simple
ingenuity to project to form a rudimentary doorhead.
Occasionally elm was used, and this was left with the edges
following the line of the trees' growth—an attractive form of
covering, which also had the advantage of bleaching to a
charming silvery grey or russet.

This type of work may be considered indigenous in Kent
and Sussex, especially near the border of the two counties,
where North-east Sussex impinges on South-west Kent—a
thickly-wooded neighbourhood in the sandy Weald extending
from Tunbridge Wells to Rye, broken into little abrupt rises
and dips where the cottages, almost all of sterling craftsmanship with finely-coloured red tile-roofs, stand beside the
winding lanes or are separated from the road by the width
of a field bounded by white palings. These weatherboardings
are painted white or light fawn colour. In this particular
neighbourhood the work is usually, though by no means
always, confined to the first storey, especially the side of the
gable, full or hipped. It is on occasion found combined, not
inharmoniously, with tilehanging, as at Groombridge (94).

There is another area of frequent and extensive weatherboarding north of the Thames, comprising some parts of
Middlesex and Hertfordshire, with South Essex up to the
middle of the county (88), and sometimes beyond (104). The
cottages here are frequently weatherboarded all over, no doubt
again for protection, but producing a slightly foreign air,
with a certain monotony of effect. The weatherboarding is
often painted white (104), but examples are found, particularly
on the seaboard of Essex, which are tarred black (88). A
curious piebald effect is produced when the weatherboarding
itself is painted a light colour and the outshut is black.

109 NOT PENNSYLVANIA, BUT BUCKMAN'S CORNER, SUSSEX

110 PLAXTOL, KENT

111 SMARDEN, KENT

KENTISH WEATHERBOARDING

112 A SYMMETRICAL RANGE OF WEATHERBOARDING AT
HAWKHURST, KENT

113   UPSHIRE, IN EPPING FOREST, ESSEX

Naturally in this district weatherboarding may be found combined with plaster, as in a fifteenth-century house at Fobbing, and the pleasant group of cottages at Little Dunmow, (*p. 37*). Occasionally weatherboarding occurs in Suffolk and Norfolk, as in the Yarmouth rows; there seems some curious connection between this practice and coastal districts. The buildings in which it is carried out *in excelsis* are the windmills throughout the country, especially in the Eastern Counties, and the enormous watermills astride the mill-streams of the quiet Suffolk rivers; similar but rather smaller examples are also to be found in the South-east. It is a matter of regret that both these classes of buildings tend to diminish. Weatherboarding is excellently adapted to the windmill, and in the case of its brethren by the water the long expanse of plain boards is frequently diversified by a picturesque jumble of gables and projecting structures, such as crane-shoots for flour sacks.

VIII

INSIDE AND AROUND THE COTTAGE

We have lingered outside the cottage, studying its construction and materials and features ; it is time for us to
cross the threshold to view the interior and see what we can
glean about the mode of life and feelings of the inmates down
the centuries. The mists of time have blurred the picture
like a badly focused screen image ; nevertheless, the faint
impressions are of the highest interest—we can witness the
first gropings of our ancestors towards comfort and well-being.
Let us not enter as the minions of a sanitary inspector or in
the spirit of a censorious health visitor ; we are present to
sympathise, not to carp or pry.

We can disregard the rudimentary structures of the Stone
Ages, and take our first glance at the dwellings of the
Glastonbury Lake village. These circular thatched huts of
wattle-and-daub, with their central hearths, were remarkably
similar to, all but identical in fact with, the beehive Kikuyu
structures in East Africa. It is hard to believe that craftsmen of the versatile skill of the Glastonbury men could not
have attained at least some slight measure of comfort, with
their utensils of corresponding fitness and grace. Passing by
the British and Saxon huts, we come to the medieval cottage
interior, where but scanty material is available from which
to draw a detailed picture. Writers from Chaucer to Bishop
Hall (*p.* 18), usually emphasise the misery of these little
hovels, yet there must have been a wider social range than
is realised among medieval country workers, from the
prosperous villein in his cottage-farm to the serf in his crude
hut. There is also the time factor to be considered ; though
change was slow, there had been an appreciable development
in conditions of rural life between A.D. 1200 and 1500. It is
obvious that the original medieval cottage was two-roomed,
whether we assume, as is more probable, that the " hall "
was living-room and kitchen combined—the " house-place "
in fact—and the " bower " a sleeping compartment, possibly
occupied by the women of the family, or whether we regard
the " hall " as a sort of stable for the beasts and the " bower "
as the living-place. Be that as it may, this two-roomed
medieval cote would strike us as grim and dark in the extreme,
a compound of draughts and smoke. The wood-fire would
be burning in the middle on a clay hearth or iron plate. A pot

114 COTTAGE STILL-LIFE, RAYDON, SUFFOLK

115　THE PRIMITIVE HEARTH OF A DONEGAL CABIN

116　THE VAST OLD HEARTH OF SHAKESPEARE'S BIRTHPLACE,
STRATFORD-ON-AVON

of stew would be simmering, and the smoke had to find its
way out through small unglazed apertures closed by wooden
shutters, or frame blinds of canvas cloth called fenestrals.

The fifteenth-century cottages from manuscript illustrations
show rudimentary dormers for ventilation, and the fireplace
is placed against the wall in one case, under a hood. The
scanty furniture would include a selection from the following :

WATTLEWORK AND THATCH OVER TWO THOUSAND YEARS AGO
AT THE GLASTONBURY LAKE VILLAGE
Reconstructed by Marjorie and C. H. B. Quennell.

a trestle table, a few roughly fashioned stools, a clothes chest,
earthenware pitchers, pots and pans, possibly a brass pot in
the case of the more well-to-do, a trivet, a skillet, a " crokke "
or iron cauldron, with wooden platters, ladles, mugs and
spoons, patiently fashioned of evenings by father and sons.
(To jump some three or four centuries, it is interesting to
compare the foregoing with the effects of a labourer at
Wenhaston, Suffolk, sold for £1. 9s. 2d. in 1681. There are
eighteen items, including " a peauter dish, two iron pottes,
a warming pan, a hatshett, a pair of Andyrons and a pele,
two brass skilletts, daubing tools, six chaires, a blanket and
two bolsters, a paire of sheetes, an old bedstead and a lether

P

bottle.") The floor would be of trodden earth, a muddy slop in wet weather, and the beds in the inner room, less smoke-blackened, would be of flock or straw, either laid on the floor or on rough wall-frames, with coarse woollen rugs for coverlets ; mattresses were highly prized, and feather-beds a precious treasure. If the mattresses were seized for some of the numerous dues, as when the Church is said to have made a ghoulish appropriation of the beds on which the dead were brought for burial, the peasants lay on heaps of straw. This scantiness of sleeping furniture seems to have been as much a matter of custom as of poverty, if we are to credit Harrison and not consider him merely an advocate of ultra-Spartan practice. His words are too well known to call for quotation here, but they seem to point to an arrangement of bed-furnishings which, if offered to convicts to-day, would cause questions in Parliament.

In such a place the cottage family lived and cooked and ate and slept, though it is probable that when weather allowed, some of the cooking was done out-of-doors. Here by the feeble light of casual rushlights the women spun and sewed and the men and boys exercised their craftsmen's skill in carving utensils and fashioning tools and farm implements, as is graphically described by Lord Ernle in his *English Farm, Past and Present* :—

Women spun and wove wool into coarse cloth, and hemp or nettles into linen ; men tanned their own leather. The rough tools required for the cultivation of the soil, and the rude house-hold utensils needed for the comforts of daily life, were made at home. In the long winter evenings, farmers, their sons, and their servants carved the wooden spoons, the platters, and the beechen bowls. They fitted and riveted the bottoms to the horn mugs, or closed, in coarse fashion, the leaks in the leathern jugs. They plaited the osiers and reeds into baskets and into " weeles " for catching fish ; they fixed handles to the scythes, rakes, and other tools ; cut the flails from holly or thorn, and fastened them with thongs to the staves ; shaped the teeth for rakes and harrows from ash or willow, and hardened them in the fire ; cut out the wooden shovels for casting the corn in the granary ; fashioned ox-yokes and bows, forks, racks and rack-staves ; twisted willows into scythe-cradles, or into traces and other harness gear. Travelling carpenters, smiths, and tinkers visited detached farmhouses and smaller villages, at rare intervals, to perform those parts of the work which needed their professional skill. Meanwhile the women plaited straw or reed for neck-collars, stitched and stuffed sheep-skin bags for cart-saddles, peeled rushes for wicks and made candles. Thread was often made from nettles. Spinning-wheels, distaff, and needles were never idle. Home-made cloth and linen

117 LODSWORTH, WEST SUSSEX

118 NEAR BARNSTAPLE, NORTH DEVON

THE COTTAGE HEARTH

120   SWIMBRIDGE, NORTH DEVON

THE COTTAGE HEARTH

119   EASHING, SURREY

supplied all wants. Flaxen linen for board-cloths, sheets, shirts, smocks or skirts, and towels, as the napkins were called, on which, before the introduction of forks, the hands were wiped, was only found in wealthy households, and on special occasions. Hemp, in ordinary households, supplied the same necessary articles, and others, such as candle-wicks, in coarser form. Shoe-threads, halters, stirrup-thongs, girths, bridles, and ropes were woven from the " carle " hemp ; the finer kind, or " fimble " hemp supplied the coarse linen for domestic use, and " hempen homespun " passed into a proverb for a countryman.

Though no doubt much of this work was carried on in medieval times, this remarkable development of home handicrafts reached its peak during the sixteenth and seventeenth centuries.

In spite of all it is difficult to feel that by 1500 the peasant of England and the adjacent countries did not manage to scrape up a certain measure of household wellbeing ; the race, like the feline, has a strong tendency to work out its own comfort, and in the picture (132) the cat, ever ease-loving, looks contented enough. A ready comparison is between the medieval cote and the " but-and-ben " or " black house " of the Western Highlands (83) and the cabins of Ireland and Wales, the latter often preserved as storehouses if new cottages have been built ; though all these are of course of solidly built stone, and no cottage of the Middle Ages approached them in stability. Personal observation shows that cottages of this same type can range from tidy comfort to squalid misery, and it is probable that in the Middle Ages also the personal equation was the greatest factor of all.

It is due to the acute observation and research of Mr. Sidney Oldall Addy* that we are largely able to reconstruct the interior arrangements of English cottages, at least in the North, at the close of the Middle Ages, and during the transition to the usual type of cottage rooms current in the seventeenth and eighteenth centuries. He had the discrimination to realise the immense interest and historic significance of quite humble buildings, which have practically without exception been swept away since he recorded them. The history of domestic buildings in England cannot be properly envisaged until some of these early fabrics have been reconstructed in suitable exhibitions or museums. The following is a brief and very inadequate summary of some of his observations.

The unit of the cruck house, the 16 feet bay, would have provided the smallest dwelling-house, but it is doubtful if a family ever submitted to such miserably meagre accommoda-

* *The Evolution of the English House*, republished 1933.

tion. The living-space could be extended by adding more
bays, by a series of built-out chambers outside the cruck
system, or by " outshuts," the latter often of boarded timber.
In a typical example in Lancashire of one bay, there was a
16 by 14 feet living-chamber, the only one with a fireplace,
called the " house-part," known further south as the " house-
place." Inside the door was a wooden screen fixture known
as the speer, which provided a serviceable interior porch;
on the inner side it could have a shelf along the top, and
occasionally a wooden settle often by the fire. Off the
house-place opened a small " buttery," or store for food and
utensils. One small chamber was built out opposite the speer,
and two from the fireplace end of the house-place, thus giving
three bedrooms, and five rooms in all, in a one-storey building.
This arrangement was on broad lines typical, though of course
the number and disposition of the rooms varied. Upper
rooms could be built above the chambers at each end, probably
reached originally by steep, sturdy ladders, which were often
replaced later by primitive stairs ; the house-place was usually
open to the roof. Thus is reached a rough and primitive form
of the central-halled yeoman's house so characteristic of Kent.
A graphic sketch of this type of structure is given by Tomber
in his *History of Blackpool* :—

I might point out a few specimens of these houses, supported
on crooks, and occasionally dignified with a porch : the interior
dark, low, open to the smoky rafters, well stored with bacon,
dried beef, etc., having a large open fireplace, over which a low,
heavy, oaken beam ran across the room, forming a sort of canopy,
beneath which was the family hearth. Opposite the fireplace
were the chamber, pronounced " chomer," and the pantry ; so
that the good housewife might overlook her store with readiness ;
nor was the " speere " or " God-speed stoop " wanting. The old
' kist ' (chest) of oak, dated wardrobe, and the door of the cupboard, opening in the wall, shone brightly, from the diligent care
and labour of the polisher's hand.

It is interesting that some of the better houses were fitted
with large carved benches and a substantial table, of such size
that they must have been constructed during the building of
the house, for their dimensions would preclude their having
being brought through door or window. This practice, with
the device of the speer, forms an early example of functional
in-built furniture, admirably adapted to the use and needs of
the occupants. Mr. Addy's researches on the development of
the chimney and fireplace are also extremely valuable. No

examples are now extant in England of the central hearth, which persisted from prehistoric dwellings to the hovels of the medieval peasant. It still, however, may be found with its stone " reredos " in the Shetlands. Apart from this lowest stratum, there was always some type of funnel to carry off the smoke, which, according to old accounts, was often built of wood, mud, or lath and plaster ; it is too much to expect, from the fragility of its construction, that any example should have survived. In many other examples a large hood or cove projected in front of the fireplace to catch the smoke, a form which in stone is to be found in many medieval castles. The remarkable fact about the cottage version of this type of fireplace was its relatively tremendous size—when carried out in brick, its lower edge was often level with the floor of the upper chamber, in which it formed an enormous tapering brick funnel, projecting into the room. If it appreciably diminished the available living-space, it would at least diffuse some heat into the fireless apartment through which it passed. The hood disappeared early from the medieval manor-house, and possibly died out similarly in cottage buildings, as it was inclined to be unstable and it was found easier to bring the whole chimney-breast forward. The staircase—at first, it is probable, merely a steep ladder giving access by a hole direct into the upper room—was later rebuilt on compact but sturdy lines around a central newel, and relegated to some convenient corner where it would occupy the least space, generally as near as possible to the chimney. The circular newel staircase has long vanished from English cottage building, and only a few timber examples of post-medieval date can be recalled in larger houses.

The regular old cottage living-room has altered little in the course of the last two or three centuries. On raising the latch and pushing open the door, we find ourselves in a low room, the ceiling crossed by heavy beams, from which may hang hams, bunches of herbs and possibly a frame for washing that can be raised or lowered. The floor is of red brick, large tiles or stone slabs, very occasionally, as in the Cotswolds, arranged in simple patterns. The window is long and low, of leaded panes with occasionally a finely wrought " cock's-comb " casement fastening ; the " prettily picturesque " diamond panes are usually an inferior nineteenth-century version. The broad window-shelf is filled with the flowering plants dear to the cottager's heart ; their gaiety more than compensates for the loss of light. There are geraniums, begonias, hydrangeas, pots of musk and a little pink flower, and occasionally a good display of botanical varieties of varied cactus plants, all carefully watered and tended, and flourishing vigorously. It is perhaps an ill-natured suggestion that this display is strategically advantageous in enabling the inhabitant to keep watch on happenings outside without being seen.

The chief feature is the fireplace, which occupies most of one side of the room; this opening, six foot or more, is spanned by an oak beam, covered by a curtained valence to increase the draught. The shelf above holds a miscellany of objects—tea canisters, a ticking wooden clock, a brass kettle, candlesticks, china toby jugs, chained dogs, a pair of simpering pottery figures or a miniature doll's house. On the raised brick hearth is an iron plate with possibly a pair of plain fire-dogs and a fire-back. The well-wrought swinging-arm pot-crane allows of several hanging pots, which can be adjusted by a ratchet and emptied by the idle-back.

It is not surprising that cottage wives now prefer the greater convenience of a range to open-fire cooking, and frequently the open fireplace has been bricked up and a kitchener inserted; occasionally an oven and small boiler have been installed on each side, leaving a small central open fire, on which the northern housewife can produce miracles of scones or girdle-cakes in an iron pan with glowing peats. By the side of the hearth are one or two inglenook seats, with a small recess to hold a glass or cup; let us not rashly follow a recent popular writer and inquire the etymology of the word ingle. These cosy warm corners are coveted in spite of their smokiness; from them you can look up the wide flue to the sky above; occasionally a window is placed at the back to light the ingle-seat. An old settle may be placed at right angles to the fireplace, occasionally backing at right angles to the door, and so serving the purpose of the speer just described. By one side of the chimneypiece may be found the bread-oven hollowed in the thickness of the wall or projecting on the outside with its little round roof of tiles or stone-slates (125); it is closed with a door of iron plate, and brushwood is burnt on its brick floor, raked out, and the bread inserted and left to bake. In a corner, or in the Cotswolds by the side of the fireplace, is a door which covers the steep straight or winding stairs to the upper floor.

There may be one or two old chairs, perhaps ladder-backed, with a Windsor armchair and a settee, a copper warming-pan,

121, 122 "ROOKERY NOOK"

123 COMPTON CHAMBERLAYNE, WILTSHIRE

124 BROADWAY, WORCESTERSHIRE

THE FRONT GARDEN

possibly an old grandfather clock, or one of the plain-faced wall type. The dresser with its display of blue china is more characteristic of Welsh cottages and is not very often found, but there may be a corner cupboard or a linen chest. The furniture, hearth, lighting utensils and household objects of old cottages have been fully recorded by the late Miss Gertrude Jekyll in her two books, *Old English Household Life* (1925), reissued under Sydney Jones's editorship in 1939, and *Old West Surrey* (1904); the collection of such objects which she made is now in the Guildford Castle Museum, and it is largely to books and local museums of this type, such as the reconstructed interiors at the Priest's House, West Hoathly, Sussex, that we must look for these remains of a past country life. Actually the old work in cottages, never very outstanding or abundant, has very largely been hunted over and cleared by dealers and collectors, who have in their turn been to some extent bamboozled by the " planting " of spurious objects for them to find. Covering the walls is the flowered wallpaper, which may on occasion spread over beams, doors (134) and everything else; in the course of generations there may be a considerable thickness from the superimposed layers. Six or seven are by no means unusual, and in one cottage in the Essex Easters *thirteen* coats of paper had actually to be stripped away before reaching the wall surface.

The pictures are a miscellaneous lot: an old sampler, perhaps, or a silhouette, chromos from Christmas numbers, a portrait of Queen Victoria or Mr. Gladstone, some of the crude German scriptural lithographs of the early nineteenth century, and brightly coloured almanacs from the church or local grocer, with, of course, several photographic groups of a weirdly garbed wedding party, a local cricket team or figures in khaki. If you are fortunate, your eyes may be gladdened by the sight of some of those intriguing lustre plaques of about a century ago. They bear stern scriptural admonitions, usually : PREPARE TO MEET THY GOD, or THOU GOD SEEST ME ! One old lady on her first night in country lodgings found a " Prepare to Meet Thy God " on each side of her bed ; after a sleepless night she left for other quarters the next morning ! There may be shelves in all sorts of odd places, holding various utensils and a few odd books, with a wireless set, quite possibly of large size with several valves, for " our Tom is a wunner for getting they furrin stations." On the other hand, with its batteries run down, it may just be an inert but admired item of household furniture.

The old cottage does not often possess the much-prized parlour, which came in with the model cottages of the mid-nineteenth century—on it Mr Pepler has written an amusing poem ; but there may be a wash-house with copper, a small larder or a scullery. Occasionally in newer cottages its floor is hollowed out to provide a bath, which it is libellously suggested by the cynical serves excellently as an indoor coal-cellar or store place for potatoes. Adjoining are the " outshuts," the sheds and outhouses which the countryman loves to multiply, a fundamental trait often forgotten by those who provide " model " cottages. This feeling can be sympathetically regarded, for there is great convenience in ample storage with limited house-room ; accommodation can then be found for a large supply of wood and coal, a perambulator, garden tools, assorted cycles, " our Bill's motor-bike," and the fowl-house.

If we go upstairs in the cottage, we shall rarely find a fire-place in one of the bedrooms, which are frequently so small that there is little space for more than beds. Sometimes in smaller cottages the further bedrooms can only be reached through the inner ones, necessitating a graded system of times for getting up. Occasionally the space at the head of the stairs is screened off into an improvised sleeping-place for one of the sons.

It remains to say a word as to the transformation which the cottage interior has often undergone at the hands of those townsfolk of a different class who have turned the building into a week-end *pied-à-terre* or permanent residence. Sometimes the change has been carried out with feeling and restraint, but it is not easy to avoid an effect of incongruity. In many cases, however, the plain rooms are overloaded with stuff that in its surroundings is bound to smack of preciousness or artificiality, and frequently the pretty-pretty effect induced can only be characterised as a regrettable degradation.

COTTAGE GARDENS

There is little space to describe the cottage gardens, which are invariably an attractive feature of the English countryside from Dan to Beersheba. It was the same in Cobbett's day, over a century ago, when he observed, " All through the country, poor as well as rich are very neat in their gardens, and very careful to raise a great variety of flowers." In them, generally speaking, the cottager and his wife manage to make the most of odd corners and limited space for a

125 A WEST COUNTRY GARDEN AT SELWORTHY, SOMERSET

126 PEMBRIDGE, HEREFORDSHIRE

127 PEMBRIDGE, HEREFORDSHIRE
THE FRONT APPROACH

burst of vivid colour and a varied display. Even the few
inches before the house-walls are turned to advantage, as may
be seen in several pictures (124, 129); at Skirmett, in the
Chilterns, the strips are made gay with forget-me-nots and
Darwin Tulips, and in the West Country are often found
little rock gardens by the threshold, bright with arabis, stone-
crop and saxifrage. Scarcely ever are the kitchen-gardens
without their flower fringes, but it is in the front space that
the family can really let itself go. The porch and walls are
covered with climbing roses, and the path to the front door
is flanked by beds edged with dwarf box, which enclose a
crowd of bright blooms from May to September—snowdrops,
daffodils, primulas, columbines, bluebells, lupins, followed by
larkspurs, lilies, snapdragons, pinks, sweet-williams, stocks,
asters and many more, with dahlias, Michaelmas daisies,
chrysanthemums to finish off the season. Rows of hollyhocks
skirt the boundary hedge, and in one corner a great old yew
overshadows the cottage well; its dark foliage makes an
effective foil to the bright flower-colours. Tennyson has
pleasantly summarised the variety of cottage flower-plots :—

> One looked all rose tree, and another wore
> A close-set robe of jasmine sown with stars ;
> This had a rosy sea of gillyflowers
> About it ; this a milky way on earth,
> Like visions in the Northern Dreamer's heavens,
> A lily avenue climbing to the doors ;
> One, almost to the martin-haunted eaves,
> A summer burial deep in hollyhocks ;
> Each its own charm. . . .

In some districts particular types of plants are seen in
special abundance : thus honesty spreads half wild over the
Chiltern places, and the gardens of Suffolk near the sea are
covered with blue and pink annual larkspurs. West Herefordshire stands out specially for its addiction to cut topiary of
box or yew, though this is also found in Northamptonshire
and other counties. In some instances, notably at Byford,
the crowded shapes are so weird that the effect is more
fantastic than attractive, but simpler forms, such as two tall
tapering yews or cypress trees beside the entrance, seen at
Sulgrave, Northamptonshire, do not fail to add a touch of
grace and distinction to the simple lay-out.

We have already spoken of the window-sills, which almost
anywhere are crowded miniature gardens of familiar or
unusual flowers. The villager will experiment with strange

Q

plants and raise them successfully from such sources as stray roots or cuttings obtained from the gardener at the Hall. He will make his own version of any outlandish names : among roses, " Gloire de Dijon " becomes " Glory-to-thee-John " ; " Général Jacquemot," " Jack-me-not " ; " Deux Ans," " Dews-Ann," while " Catillac " stewing pears have appeared as " Cattle-axe."

Distributed throughout the country are famous pleasances and private gardens, many of which, it has been arranged, can be seen by the public at stated times for a small payment devoted to a nursing fund. But these, of necessity, are secluded in wide parks, away from the gaze of the casual passer-by. The little gardens, insignificant singly but impressive and effective by their uncounted number, are visually the common property of all, and an endless joy and pleasure to the beholder. It is due to them that the countryside, in all but the blighted industrial districts, wears from February to November a gay multi-coloured mantle of bright flowers, changeful but unfailing.

TOPIARY-WORK IN A COTTAGE GARDEN, STRETTON SUGWAS,
HEREFORDSHIRE

Drawn by Sydney R. Jones.

IX

COTTAGE FOLK

It is impossible to leave the old cottage without glancing very briefly and superficially at the people who dwell in it and the life unfolded within its walls. After all, whether attractive or squalid, the cottage is the setting for an agelong human drama which only stays its course when the structure is destroyed or falls into ruin. With a few exceptions, the country cottager has received somewhat scant treatment at the hands of writers of books or plays. It has become almost too commonplace for novelists to chronicle the vicissitudes of a family, through any period up to a century, in a " saga," which may be an acute piece of psychological analysis, grimly realistic, or merely desperately dull ; but no author, so far as the writers' acquaintance with recent literature allows, has taken for his theme the chequered fortunes of the dwellers in an old cottage during the whole or any part of the three to four hundred years of its habitation. The thought has been well expressed by Rider Haggard in *A Farmer's Year* :—

Oh! if only the place (a cottage on Baker's Farm, Bedingham, Norfolk) could tell all its story, with the detail necessary to make us understand it, what a story that would be! A humble tale perhaps—a tale of little things and obscure lives and yet how fascinating ! When we consider bygone ages we are apt to dwell only upon the histories of distinguished individuals and the records of great and startling occurrences. Yet those do not really make up the past. Notable men are rare; there be very few in any age who can lift their heads and voices high enough above the raving crowd for the world to see and hear them, and great events occur only from time to time. But behind these Titans existed the dim multitudes of the people—those whose qualities and characters really fashioned the nation for good or ill; our forefathers, whose instincts and strivings built up the empire we inherit, in whom lay the weight and influence which brought about the revolutions of our history and from whom were produced those strong characters that carried out their will, and with whose names we are still familiar. But of all these forgotten humble hordes there remains nothing but ourselves, who, by the mysterious descent of blood, continue their existence, and such poor memorials as are inscribed by some long-dead hand upon the imperishable stone.

A microcosm of human life has been lived within those little walls in the course of some four centuries of continuous habitation. It is hard to visualise the contribution of one country cottage alone to the course of national life, or to imagine the appearance and character of the goodly company of old and young that would assemble, had we the power to recall those who had dwelt within it.   In the course of some fifteen generations probably two hundred folk could claim it as their one-time house ;   all the gamut of human emotions has been displayed there :   simple nobility, endurance and contentment, against which can be ranged discontent, wretchedness, jealousy and despair.   Many children have there seen the light, and older folk there drawn their last breath, while its boys and girls have gone forth to serve their country in distant lands, or to help sustain the vast industrial machinery of the towns.

The annals of lonely hamlets are by no means always peaceful and humdrum, as it was easy to realise standing with a vicar's wife in a remote churchyard on the Welsh Border.   The small red-brick Georgian church lay in a green cup and used to be called " in the Hole," and the hilly little cemetery was nearly full of graves, though they were but few. She was a bright, keen-witted, elderly woman, with a turn of incisive speech.   " Yes," she said, " that mound is of the little girl who was burned to death at the Upper Wood Farm ; I think she might have survived if she had been properly treated in time."   She continued briskly :   " Over there lies Jim Burrows ;   he was a porter at the junction after his army service, and was swept away when bathing in the river.   The current is very treacherous at the bend, and he had been warned against it ;   I rather think he was drunk at the time. That grave is of an oldish man we found lying by the road-side late one autumn.   We did what we could for him, but he was half-frozen and did not recover consciousness.   We never knew his name."   She did not know that hers was soon to be a tragic enough passing to the little churchyard, with an inquest in the old vicarage she had inhabited so long.   In curious contrast with these violent tales, one could read the epitaphs on most of the tombstones, stating " Her end was peace," and so on, while one mentioned " robes of shining innocence "—which were, perhaps, scarcely in accord with the local illegitimacy statistics.   One, however, ended on a note of utter disillusionment, struck by an elderly married lady :

" Farewell affliction, grief, and pain—
Welcome eternal bliss ;
Thank God I ne'er can live again
In such a world as this."

128 SUNDAY AFTERNOON

129 SUMMER MORNING AT SNOWSHILL, GLOUCESTERSHIRE

The cottager need owe no debt of gratitude to medieval society; if the precise status of his existence is, and most probably must remain, to some extent a matter of controversy, it is likely that his conditions of life and service, even when improved and mitigated, would be found intolerable by the worst-off slum-dweller in a depressed area to-day. A carefully drawn picture of a medieval peasant family's Sunday is drawn by Mr. H. S. Bennett in his excellent study of *Life on the English Manor*.

The society of later centuries dispossessed the peasant with cynical indifference of his traditional rights in the land, but it continued to regulate his private life with almost feudal rigour for many years. It is curious that this life has never received adequate treatment in its country's literature, and that the great book on the subject remains to be written. First came a batch of Early Victorian sob-stuff, in which the cottager's daughter died slowly of a " decline," resigned to the will of heaven, with profuse pietistic moralisings. This was succeeded by the pessimistic or realistic school of Thomas Hardy, Mary Webb and *The Shropshire Lad*, in which the countryman was represented as the sport of a malignant fate. Extreme cases form an English version of the Russian school in which, as a humorist has remarked, psychological meanderings grow ever more involved, until the moujik commits suicide on page 346. Too often this school shows the countryman as a humourless creature, which he certainly is not. Hardy's Wessex Novels, despite their preoccupation with the eternities, give a pleasant and accurate picture of a country life largely passed away, but some more recent writers tend to show the cottager as a sort of slow-minded clown or buffoon. It is a relief to come across a collection of straightforward stories in which the labourer figures as a normal human being, such as those of Mr. A. E. Coppard, Mr. Adrian Bell, Mr. A. G. Street, Mr. H. E. Bates, or Miss Doreen Wallace.

The life of a country hamlet is a sealed book to the majority of present-day Englishmen, who are inveterate townsmen, and little can be said here to give an adequate picture of it. But in truth the country labourer is in reality an ordinary Englishman, no different from the rest of us, so far as it is feasible to generalise about any class. To strike an average, possibly somewhat hypothetical, the agricultural worker is usually pleasant and friendly, with that spontaneous kindliness that distinguishes the man who lives close to nature. If his " book-larnin " may be slight, he is usually exceedingly

R

shrewd, resourceful and knowledgeable on all matters connected with his work or coming within his personal observation ; he is rather keener on his job than the town worker
and less " cursed with the intense selfishness of the lower
classes." The experienced farm-worker is highly skilled in a
variety of tasks, and in much that he does has nowadays to be
a quick and ready mechanic. He has a real pride in his job ;
on a Sunday morning at the Bull and Butcher, at Turville
in the Chilterns, an ancient labourer proudly recounted his
skill at hedging, ditching and the rest of his jobs, while a
gang of ribald cyclists, to rag him, suggested that his prowess
principally consisted in the emptying of pint pots. The old
fellow's annoyance was almost frenzied, and it took much
soothing on the part of some older men to pacify him with
the assurance that the value of his work was understood and
appreciated.

Nevertheless, the cottager has never lacked for champions.
The familiar phrases of Gray's *Elegy* represent an early, if
somewhat romanticised, endeavour to set forth the pathos of
these obscure lives, narrow and restricted, on the threshold of
one of the worst periods of agricultural depression. Crabbe
did not mince his words in favour of the rural worker, and
Cobbett, hard-hitting old great-heart, cried : " The Labourer,
was I to have no feeling for him ? " Sympathy and under-
standing are to be found in the writings of Richard Jefferies,
Rider Haggard, Gertrude Jekyll and others down to the
anonymous author of *England's Green and Pleasant Land*. But it
is Kipling, in his poem, " The Land " (*A Diversity of Creatures*)
who has rightly claimed for the field worker that he is the
real owner of the English Country, *par droit* if never *par loi*,
since he is the master craftsman who has transformed its landscape and created the green garden which is England to-day :—

> His dead are in the churchyard—thirty generations laid,
> Their names went down in Domesday Book when
>   Domesday Book was made
> And the passion and the piety and prowess of his line,
> Have seeded, rooted, fruited, in some land the Law calls
>   mine.
>
> *   *   *   *   *   *
>
> He is bailiff, woodman, wheelwright, field surveyor,
>   engineer,
> And if flagrantly a poacher,—'tain't for me to interfere.
>
> *   *   *   *   *   *

131 THE COTTAGER FALLEN ON EVIL DAYS.
By Jean Bourdichon, *circa* 1500

130 COTTAGES AT WILTON IN THE SIXTEENTH
CENTURY. From the Pembroke Survey

132 COTTAGE LIFE IN WINTER IN THE SIXTEENTH CENTURY.
From the Grimani Breviary

—" Hev it jest as you've a mind to, but . . ."—and so he
    takes command,
For whoever pays the taxes old Mus' Hobden owns the
    land.

There are two major tragedies of the English countryside
to-day—the first is that it is peopled largely with human stock
that has been subjected to a severe drain. The wretched conditions and meagre opportunities of country life and work have
meant that for a century past the most active and enterprising
of its young people have been forced to migrate into the
towns, and the pick of the country population is thus permanently lost to the land. No effective measures have been
advised for checking this migration, in itself a source of
national danger. The second tragedy is the pitiable plight of
the old labourer when advancing age has sapped his strength
for active work. " What's there to look forward to now I
am getting on in years ? " is the tragic cry of the elderly
worker whose strength is slipping from him, often wholly or
partially crippled by rheumatism or touched by paralysis.
If he is not a widower, his wife is as old as himself, perhaps
ailing or invalid ; very likely the children they have struggled
to bring up are overseas, or cluttered with heavy family cares
of their own, or callously refuse to help their parents. The
old folks can struggle on with double Old Age Pensions, but
forlorn is the lot of the old man by himself ; his cottage is
nearly always coveted for a younger man and his family.
One fine old shepherd is recorded to have said : " It were
fair bondage ; it were a bondage," of his lifetime of unceasing
ill-paid toil, as he lay " wore out, wore out utterly, mortil
weary and wishful for the end."

Nevertheless, in spite of hard and ill-paid work and few of
the recreations and distractions which we think essential to
our existence, it would be a mistake to imagine that the
average farm-worker, even when elderly, poverty-stricken and
ailing, fails to enjoy life and achieve a fair measure of happiness.
Frequently he is a fine exemplification of the fundamental
aphorism of Scripture, that " a man's life consisteth not in the
abundance of the things which he possesseth." He retains a
keen interest in life, with its endless petty details of what to
us would be a wearisome monotony, and his quiet humour and
steadfast cheerfulness can be unfailing, and put to shame the
grumbles of those endowed with far more material blessings.
He can find contentment in the bare indispensables of life,

and peace in the narrow circle of an unchanging daily round. The countryman in fact may be said to have kept down the centuries that spirit of spontaneous yet quietly joyous gaiety which was, if it is no longer, the most distinctive and out-standing characteristic of the English people, and has expressed itself in the music of their great centuries. His outlook is as cheery as it is philosophic; undaunted by the lack of much that to the town-dweller makes life worth living, his spirit is unquenched, his head unbowed, and of many of his class it can be said that, beyond a doubt, they are very gallant gentlemen.

From the Middle Ages the cottager's chief burden has been the unwieldy size of his excessive family. Langland, who in *Piers Plowman* classes the cottager among the desperately unfortunate of life, has shown his insight in a passage of bitter pathos :—

> The neediest are our neighbours if we give heed to them,
> Prisoners in the dungeon, the poor in the cottage,
> Charged with a crew of children and with a landlord's rent.
> What they win by their spinning to make their porridge with,
> Milk and meal, to satisfy the babes,
> The babes that continually cry for food—
> This they must spend on the rent of their houses ;
> Aye, and themselves suffer with hunger,
> With woe in winter, rising a-nights
> In the narrow room to rock the cradle.
> Pitiful is it to read the cottage women's woe,
> Aye, and many another that puts a good face on it,
> Ashamed to beg, ashamed to let neighbours know
> All that they need, noontide and evening.
> Many the children, and nought but a man's hands
> To clothe and feed them ; and few pennies come in,
> And many mouths to eat the pennies up.
> Bread and thin ale for them are a banquet,
> Cold flesh and cold fish are like roast venison ;
> A farthing's worth of mussels, a farthing's worth of cockles,
> Were a feast for them, on Friday or fast-days ;
> It were charity to help these that be at heavy charges,
> To comfort the cottager, the crooked and the blind.

The cottager's wife has often been accused of being a shiftless housekeeper, but what prodigies of managing, what heights of skimping and scraping, what infinity of toil were needed to bring up eight to twelve children on thirteen shillings a week. And yet it was done ; except in a few slatternly households, the boys and girls were tolerably well fed and clothed, and went out to take their active part in the world's work. In the nineteenth century it was regarded as inevitable that the field worker's family should be of this stupendous extent, and *Devonshire Idylls* tells tales of the heroic struggle without any idea that it was a wasteful and unneeded one. Now, for the younger generation at least, has come emancipation from this agelong bondage, and the labourer's enormous families are gone for good, in spite of Anglo-Catholic denunciations and other reactionary influences. Knowledge of family regulation has come to stay, and already the pendulum has swung so far that there is a shortage of boy labour on some East Anglian farms. It is only just in time, for the ploughman with a round dozen of children in a cottage of painfully inadequate accommodation might well find himself in trouble under a recent Overcrowding Act, though it be administered with merciful laxity by some rural authorities. If hailed by some as a splendid measure of social reform, no more admirable instrument could have been devised for the discouragement of families of any size, after which the Government seems now somewhat belatedly to be hankering.

Many of the cottages are by no means desirable habitations, as the writer of *England's Green and Pleasant Land* is at pains to point out. He speaks of the leaky unceiled roofs, damp floors, water supply at a standpipe and the meagre sanitation of a stinking privy. To reach either of these last two inconveniences may often involve crossing the road. And yet, " the cottages, with all their defects, have inside a look and feeling of comfort. They are damp in places only. They are not cold. There are no draughts. The firesides are snug, the small, low-ceilinged living-rooms cosy. And everything is clean and trim."

Yet in these defective dwellings a fine race has been reared, whose members have often lived to a ripe old age. It is surely absurd to condemn a building for what are often purely technical defects, and have it pulled down at a time of great shortage of country accommodation. One prominent member of the Labour Party, if he is not misreported, would pull down every old cottage in the country because it does not incorporate a damp course. There is too much haste to get a magistrate's order for demolition, which cannot be rescinded when once made. It may flatter the self-importance of petty officialdom ; but there is too much of the law of the Medes and Persians about what are after all remarkably fallible proceedings, such as the case of a paternity order which could not be rescinded though the proceedings by which it was obtained were admittedly founded on perjury.   Sometimes busybody-wiseacres among local authorities care little about the comfort and convenience of the inhabitants of the buildings they condemn, and the effect of ill-judged and hastily drafted measures of so-called social reform often tend to increase the misery of the aged, the ailing and the feeble.   It is a cause for thankfulness that there is now a certain amount of reconditioning, private and subsidised, of the old fabrics, but it needs encouragement and extension, and superior authorities should veto the insistence for demolition in which some petty-minded councils indulge, when owners are prepared to spend liberally on reconditioning.   The suggested destruction of a large proportion of the adorable village of Finchingfield, Essex is a national calamity which should be held up to general execration.

The countryman is usually friendly to visitors and " casual-mets," but those who go to live in his district must expect to find themselves regarded as " foreigners " till after a decade or so of steady " digging-in."   Some villages have a definitely poisonous atmosphere, and a faithful record of their sayings and doings in play or novel would seem a wildly overstated exaggeration.   Take the case of an elderly, well-to-do couple who settled in a Home Counties' village.   As the usual gambit it was given out that the wife was not married to the husband.   She was not Mrs. Williams, just " the Woman at Hillside."   In consequence, a virtuous housemaid gave notice.   The blacksmith's son, engaged as chauffeur, issued an ultimatum that there was to be no driving after 6 P.M., Saturday afternoon or Sunday.   The postman opened their letters, and from a misunderstanding of their contents attempted a clumsy sort of blackmail, for which he was sentenced to hard labour at the local assizes.   The postmistress habitually listened in to telephone conversations; on one occasion a London friend waxed rather confidential, and the husband said warningly, " You had better be careful what you say; they always tap the wire at the Post Office." An indignant feminine voice on the air interposed, " How dare you say such a thing; I'm sure I've never done anything of the sort ! "

Gossip is the curse of village and country-town life; as a sympathetic first-hand chronicler writes : " The hamlet is corroded with uncharitableness, the pettiest feuds and jealousy, paltry snobberies and trumpery vanities." *   There have been

* *England's Green and Pleasant Land.*

133   THE COTTAGE FIRESIDE, *circa* 1800.   By W. R. Bigg, R.A.

134   THE COTTAGE FIRESIDE IN SUFFOLK TO-DAY

135 A COTTAGE CATSLIDE, STEYNING, SUSSEX

136 WAITING FOR MASTER: Twyning Green, Gloucestershire

several glaring instances of this strife of tongues lately, in one of which the poor victim, a middle-aged spinster whose ill-health was ascribed to pregnancy, committed suicide. Gossip is a perverted attempt at self-expression, a form of malicious *Schadenfreude*, an endeavour to bring a thrill into dull and petty lives, which it seems nothing will eradicate. Some communities, however, have a dread of gossip and apply the effective home-made remedy of a stern boycott of those addicted to it. It was thus only by chance that a chronicler found in Hurstbourne Tarrant, Hampshire, the reason why the lodgers from one cottage invariably flitted at Michaelmas. The queer old woman who lived in it kept bees and drank home-made mead from their honey. She lived upstairs and let the ground-floor, but had bored holes through the ceiling, and spent much of her time lying prone with her eye to the peephole, observing the domestic life of the family below. The lodgers always departed as soon as they discovered that they were spied upon, but never told. The " poison-pen " anonymous-letter manifestation is merely another form of this unpleasant tendency, and many painful cases, as recently reported, have found their way into the courts. A spiritual transformation, a " change of heart," combined with psychological treatment, seems indicated.

Though the village may be free and easy enough about happenings before marriage, it is usually quite strict about anything afterwards, and divorce among cottage-dwellers is almost unknown. Offenders are, or used to be, punished by " rough music "—a trail of chaff would be laid to the door of the cottage where there was a suspected case of wife-beating, to announce that " There is thrashing going on here." If this warning was disregarded, the men and boys made a hideous din by beating pans, kettles and tin cans. At one vicarage, the elderly clergyman, a scholar of note, ran a small " coaching " establishment; the village, with the usual bias of gossip, imagined that he was too familiar with the governess who taught the younger boys, and treated him to a dose of " rough music." The vicar, a rather grim, austere man, took the matter to his bishop, who assured him that he must regard it as his " cross," and nothing could be done except to live down the slandering of evil tongues. In Yorkshire, boys and men made " rough music " while two rode on a pole carried on their companions' shoulders outside the door where the wife henpecked the husband; it was called " riding the stang."

There are several recent innovations which have done much, and will do more, to ameliorate the country dweller's lot, and may even serve as a drag to slow down the infiltration to the towns. The motor omnibus, wireless and " the pictures " are potent forces against the twin devils of monotony and isolation. The motor bus is an unmixed blessing; people can shop in the big town, or visit friends at a distance formerly impossible. Specially late omnibuses are in peace time run back to even remote places for the convenience of Saturday picture-goers, and coaches are hired for games, club journeys or outings of all kinds of bodies. The pictures are a fine escapist medium, and wireless keeps all who can afford it in touch with the world at large. Then there are dances, whether held in the nearest town or the village hall, itself a centre for talks and gatherings, and the varied activities of the Women's Institutes, whose stimulating programmes of lectures, classes, discussions and outings, are also helping to spread the practice of helpful handicrafts. Even A.R.P., with its sense of combined effort, is a distraction, though it is quaint to find Instruction in Air Raid Precautions in Toller Porcorum !

And so we must take leave of that fine worker and master craftsman, the village labourer. Much remains to be done for his lot by the country of which he has deserved so well, and which has so consistently oppressed or neglected him. Wages are now better—provided agriculture can afford to pay them. His inclusion in the unemployment insurance scheme may be of some little benefit, and, in addition to these decided ameliorations, he has his garden and allotment, church services and festivals, flower and fruit shows, club or choir outings. A wider recognition is necessary of the extent of England's heritage in her old cottages and the sturdy country stock that dwell in them. For both heritages are wasting and in jeopardy ; the cottages are being destroyed, the folk leaving the country. It is for England to foster, cherish and preserve them both. If she is unworthy, they will both, to her permanent detriment, vanish from the face of the land.

137 IN THE VILLAGE STREET, GRANTCHESTER, CAMBRIDGESHIRE

138 WHITEWASHED BRICK AT HEMINGFORD, HUNTINGDONSHIRE

139 NEAR BRAMPTON, SUFFOLK

140 NEAR LEATHERHEAD, SURREY

VETERANS OF 1815: from Engravings by Francis Stevens

X

THE LATER COTTAGE: CONCLUSION

In the year 1815, in spite of the distractions of the Hundred Days, a Mr. Francis Stevens produced, with what success there is now no means of tracing, a volume of *Views of Cottages and Farmhouses in England and Wales, etched from the Designs of the most Celebrated Artists.* " This work," he informed his public in an introduction, " affords a specimen of domestic architecture in every county in England and Wales ; the variety of form and simplicity of design which are comprised in the subjects, the distribution of light and shadow, and the freedom of execution which the style of etching exhibits, it is presumed, may yield instruction to the amateur of painting, and amusement to those who delight in contemplating the rural beauties of our isle."

The " rural beauties " had, indeed, been in the air for some time past, but they were as yet seldom considered complete without an element of melancholy introduced in the form of some gaunt and weed-tufted ruin, some abandoned fane, to satisfy the romantic cravings of an appetite to find such rich satiety in *The Waverley Novels.* Goldsmith, in 1770, had, of course, struck a more domestic note in his *Deserted Village,* but even so, Stevens' idea was something of a novelty, for few can then have associated romantic melancholy with the plight of the old cottages, now falling into disuse and dilapidation on every hand. Here, indeed, was an almost endless theme for the musings of the poetaster and the facile brush of the maiden lady, and one to which Stevens did ample justice in his valuably detailed and occasionally beautiful plates. Nevertheless, turning the pages of his book, one cannot but wonder at the callousness of an age which found, in the wholesale ruin of the traditional architecture of its country-side, only a stimulus to the " enlightening radii of taste," of which, as the author was constrained to point out, " our dignified clergy and other learned schoolmen have for ages acted as the preceptors."

Collectively, these plates form an almost perfect background to the drama of malnutrition, rick-burning and transportation which formed one of the many grim little curtain-raisers to the Victorian epic ; a background of gaping walls, tumble-down fences and decayed thatch, mingling in a kind of romantic bedragglement with wraith-like children and skinny

S   105

beasts (139, 140). We have been able in some cases to compare
the engraved subjects with modern photographs of a few of
the buildings which have survived by some fluke, and it would
not seem possible that they could have outlived such dilapidation. The causes for the state of affairs illustrated by
Stevens have been discussed earlier in this book, and there is
no need to go into them again. For present purposes it will
suffice that the decay of rural life that set in around 1770
was, on the whole, observed with cynical indifference by the
landed classes, whose interest in their tenants was by now apt
to stop short of keeping their roofs weathertight or their
walls standing. It speaks for the stoutness of the cottage
fabrics that they have so frequently survived a whole epoch
of neglect, and can still be reconditioned for a further long
term of service—though to this period must be ascribed the
disappearance of innumerable cob cottages, once common
throughout the country, but now rare except in the South-
west, for the material crumbles in a comparative twinkling
once it loses its thatch covering.

There were landlords and landlords, of course, and from
the eighteenth century the " model village " became a fairly
frequent adjunct of the great house, for the accommodation
of the estate servants and labourers. Sometimes it was found
that the old cottages obtruded too closely on the calm of the
lawns and vistas, as was the case at Milton Abbas, Dorset,
where, when the Abbey was enlarged about 1750, Lord
Dorchester demolished the village and laid out a new one
further away; laid it out so attractively, moreover, that
Milton Abbas, with its long street climbing gently between
woods, and its symmetrically grouped cottage couples, each
separated by a plot of land and a chestnut tree, is now, in its
maturity, one of the most delightful things of its kind in the
country (141). Other schemes of the later eighteenth century
were Lowther in Westmorland, a really impressive piece of
village planning in the yellow local stone, with a reserved
classic air (142), and Harewood in Yorkshire, with its great
avenue, less consistent in lay-out, but containing some
attractive groups in which Robert Adam may have had a
hand.

Villages such as these were probably conceived rather to
improve the approaches to a great house than from any
particular solicitude for the inhabitants, whom, at the same
time, the estate would provide with safe and sufficient employment while the requisite standard of formal servility was

141 MILTON ABBAS, DORSET (*circa* 1750): the perfect Model Village

142 LOWTHER, WESTMORLAND: an effective late-Georgian
Housing Scheme

143 COLESHILL, BERKSHIRE: Victorian Jacobean

144   ICKWELL, BEDFORDSHIRE

145   OLD WARDEN, BEDFORDSHIRE

MODEL COTTAGES OF THE EARLY NINETEENTH CENTURY

146 "STEWARD'S COTTAGE"

147 "COTTAGE ADAPTED TO GARDEN SCENERY"
From Papworth's *Rural Residences*, 1818

maintained. It is not certain when the term " model village "
first came to be applied, but it is redolent of the moral
snobbery, bullying philanthropy and garbled romanticism of
the age that succeeded the Georgian. Its neat confusion of
thatch, its tiled chimneys and casement windows—the hollyhocks peeping above clipped hedges and the rambler-roses
twining the bark porches—formed a perfect setting for the
besmocked and sunbonneted rustics, who touched their fore-
locks or bobbed their curtseys as the bombazine Lady Bountiful,
basket on arm, bustled her way down the village street on her
errand of mercy. It is a style of architecture whose very
bogusness is now its chief charm. One of its earliest apostles
was J. B. Papworth, the architect of Cheltenham, who, in his
book on *Rural Residences . . . consisting of Designs for Cottages,
Decorated Cottages, Small Villas and other Ornamental Buildings*,
published in 1818, expatiated on the advantages of more
picturesque houses for the labouring poor. " Of these humble
dwellings," he wrote, " the character, or style, cannot be
too simple ; the ornaments which fancy in her playful mood
may suggest, ill associate with the modest and moderate claims
of this respectable and useful class of society ; the symbols
of ease and luxury are incongruous with the labourer's busy
life and frugal means, and ought therefore to be omitted ;
but a gracefulness of form and proportion is as applicable to
this edifice as to the mansion, and there are also genuine
embellishments belonging to the cottage of the British labourer,
which if denied, an important source of rural beauty has lost
its best sentiment with its greatest charm ; the broken casement, the patched wall, the sunken roof, the hatch unhinged,
the withered shrub, are corresponding testimonials of the
husbandman's relaxed energies and broken spirit. The porch
in which he rests after the fatigues of the day, ornamented
by some flowering creeper, at once affords him shade and
repose ; neatness and cleanliness, connected with these and
other means of external cheerfulness, bespeak that elasticity of
mind, and spring of action, which produce industry and
cheerfulness, and demonstrate that peace and content at least
dwell with its inhabitants."

The model village, sprouting mushroom-fashion in a wilder-
ness of agricultural depression and rural misery, was, indeed,
not the least attractive fake of an, in many ways, superficial
period ; and even to-day it is remarkable how its Christmas-
calendar prettiness can attract the more gullible droves of
tourists. Old Warden, Bedfordshire, built by Samuel Whit-

bread, of Southill, in the early nineteenth century, is a complete and disarming example (145), as is its neighbour, Ickwell (144), snuggling around a green on which they have preserved the maypole dances. Little Bredy, Dorset, in its delicious combe, forms a pretty complement to its Gothick hall, and there are many more of them, one of the most attractive being Coleshill, Berkshire, where, despite a house in the manner of Inigo Jones, the cottages are in a spiky version of " Jacobean " (143). Beyond such complete villages, the Papworth idea found much individual favour throughout the countryside, and can be seen expressed in many an isolated " cottage adapted to park scenery," or " *cottage orné* adapted to romantic scenery " on the great estates, to say nothing of the rose-clad dairies, oval entrance lodges and casemented keepers' cottages, with chimneys of diapered tiles and scalloped thatches, which are almost numberless. At Rendlesham in Suffolk there are even pseudo-Gothic chapter-houses as lodges, and it is curious to see the chimney-smoke issuing from the topmost pinnacles.

This was a form of building that appealed to the richer landlord throughout the nineteenth century and even after, though the model villages of the 'seventies or 'eighties, such as Tring and Waddesden on the Rothschild estates, with their fretted bargeboards, bogus timbering and lurid brick, can be of a hideousness and incongruousness that would be hard to equal. A pretty village " improved " in this manner is Wimborne St. Giles, Dorset, where an Anglo-Catholic delirium has overtaken the decent seventeenth-century church ; and some later buildings on the adjoining Crichel estate are in much the same manner. On the other hand, half-timber cottages of exceptionally good design were erected at Penshurst, Kent, some few years earlier by George Devey.

Brick, used with such happy effect during the earlier periods for special features such as mullions or chimneys, was, with the eighteenth century, to find its way into nearly every village, breaking the time-honoured congruity of the local materials. During the Middle Ages, and for some time after, it was largely imported, and thus beyond the means of smaller buildings ; but the lesson learnt from the Great Fire of 1666, which seems to have caused the most considerable drift from timber-framing, was responsible for the establishment of a brick industry, with certain distinguishable varieties of colour and bond, in most parts of the country. Beyond the major advantage of fireproofing, the wider use of brick from now on, or of stone in districts where there was a ready supply,

148 DIAPERED BRICKWORK AT GROOMBRIDGE, KENT

149   BUCKLERS HARD, HAMPSHIRE

150   ELMLEY CASTLE, WORCESTERSHIRE

COTTAGE ROWS IN GEORGIAN BRICK

had another important effect in dealing a blow to the rats and
other vermin which had infested the timbered houses, causing
a steady drain on the resources of the housewife, and periodi-
cally disseminating disease and plague through the communities
they attacked.

Though the first appearance of brick in the village was
generally limited to the more substantial houses, by the
eighteenth century it was no rarity to find it also employed
for cottages, at first with a pleasant delicacy of effect and some
attempt at detail in moldings, doorheads, cornices and the
like. One device which lent variety to both colour and
texture was the use of purplish vitrified headers—a practice
fairly usual in eighteenth-century building. It was a variant
of the old Tudor method of diapered brickwork, and was in
general effective. But when, unlike sixteenth-century practice,
the whole front was chequered with the two types of brick, as
at Groombridge (148), the result was a rather staring restless-
ness, hardly preferable to the monotony which it was intended
to avoid.

It was not in most cases until after the agrarian decline
that followed Waterloo that the material began to be employed
wholesale in certain parts of the country, more particularly in
the Central and Northern Midlands, where the box-like
growth of featureless brick cottages, singly or in couples,
groups and rows, spread from the new industrial districts
like a red and yellow fungus over the countryside. Probably,
if a census of cottage materials were undertaken, it would
now be found that brick easily outnumbers the rest; and in
such a district as East Anglia, with a good brickwork tradition,
it would be a mistake to depreciate its numerous examples of
sound building. But they rarely show anything of mark in
the way of detail or features, and commend themselves only
by their happy effects of colour and texture. White- or
colour-washing of brick walls is fairly common in various
districts and is not objectionable; but some curious effects
occur when the brick-red begins to show through in patches.

From here it is but a step to the mean little " council
houses," which seem nowadays to perch with such malevolent
intention to spoil the patch of country in which they stand,
the gabled " villas " of the village fringes, and those later
" bungalows " whose flushed asbestos roofs lend such disharmony to the venerable rustic half-tones. The unstemmed
tide of dingy-blue Welsh slates over the roofs has created
another and very widespread eyesore. Their substitution for

T

the old tiles, stone-slates or thatch has already ruined the
distant views of most of our towns, and is beginning to ruin
the villages, too, as one realised the other day, looking down
on the old houses of Abbotsbury from the St. Catherine's
Chapel knoll. Inoffensive in itself by its very mediocrity,
theirs is a colour that achieves a supreme disharmony in
almost every English landscape. How one longs nowadays,
when moving about the country, to sweep away the little
of the last hundred years or so, the " council houses," the
" villas " and the " bungalows "; to tear down the Welsh
slates and the asbestos " tiles," and restore to the solid nuclei
of our villages something of that time-honoured seemliness in
colour, texture and design achieved by many centuries of
quiet usage, and destroyed by the incontinence of one !

That much still remains to us of our cottage heritage in
every English district will be apparent to anyone glancing
through the illustrations that accompany these pages. It is
true that, in many cases, the domestic amenities these little
buildings have to offer are frugal in the extreme in comparison with those of the standardised dwellings which are
springing up on every hand ; yet few will deny that, in their
unobtrusive way, the old cottages are often a determining
factor in the beauty of the countryside, or that with their
disappearance the landscape would lose one of its most vital
ingredients. Liberal schools of thought are apt to jeer at a
sentiment that would preserve the outworn and antique rather
than provide an efficient mass-produced substitute for the
housing of our rural population ; yet liberal thought is always
the first to demand the preservation of the countryside as a
kind of " national garden," and will take up the challenge
hotly enough when private or public interests threaten its
integrity or beauties. One may think of the recent outcries
that followed the sequestration of the downland behind
Lulworth Cove by the War Office as a training-ground for
tanks, and the threat to the Abbotsbury swans when the
Chesil Bank was given over to gunnery practice ; yet these
measures have probably saved the two districts from a
vulgarisation far more distasteful than could result from the
occasional crash of high explosive or the drone of tanks.
The liberal attitude, though well-meaning, is apt to be illogical
in these matters, and we would suggest to that section of the
Press which is always, to its credit, ready to take up the
cudgels in defence of some threatened national beauty, that a
less spectacular, but more useful, purpose could be achieved

by a nation-wide " crusade," of the type favoured by news-papers with a circulation around the million mark, backed with publicity and money, to rehabilitate the old cottage fabrics for modern use, employing something of the careful scholarship that has lately been bestowed on ancient monu-ments by bodies from the Office of Works down. In most cases it probably takes more money to salve an old cottage in this way than to pull it down and substitute a " bungalow " ; but we feel convinced that, if the matter were put to it from the right angle, the interested public, already large and rapidly growing, would come to the rescue with practical enthusiasm.

Private enterprise has already done much to save old houses in the country and fix them up as comfortable " week-end cottages "—though the buildings in question are more often abandoned farms or yeomen's houses. Sometimes the work is done with sympathy and taste, but more often the results are so appalling that one feels that it would have been better for the buildings to have met an honourable end than to have bought their respite at the expense of such vulgarity. " I want to find a Tudor cottage in Sussex," the editress of a " ladies' journal " told us the other day at lunch ; " just a beautiful shell to be *gutted*." Her remark set us thinking of the Sunday afternoons of actresses and popular novelists beneath the striped umbrellas : tea, talk and cocktails, with a glimpse of tortured half-timber through the rambler roses. We thought of the black-beamed interiors, the bottle-glass windows (with here and there a " stained " pane from a cathedral city antique shop), the copper warming-pans, the orange chintzes, the faked oak furniture, the willow-pattern plates and the " old pewter." We thought of the immortal stage-set for that immortal play, "Rookery Nook," and began to long for the clear-cut lines, the metallic emptiness of an interior by Le Corbusier. Taste and discrimination in these matters are, alas, the exception rather than the rule, and the cult of the antique, that pipe-dream of the earlier Romantics, has all but petered out in a Surrey lane and a Tottenham Court Road junkshop.

To-day, the mere *cult* of the antique, however intellectualised or rarified, is not enough. The beauty of our landscape has always been of slow growth, each generation adding its fresh deposit to the rich sweet mould. That our own uneasy age will leave its quota to posterity we may still believe and hope ; nevertheless this quota, in the English scheme of things, will lose much of its value unless it can be compounded with what has come before and what comes after. Mass-production *needs* the help of tradition if it is to achieve the unshaken fundamentals of " commodity, firmness and delight " propounded by Sir Henry Wootton, and given such sterling semblance by the older handcrafts; and of the three, the first seems the only one in which we have so far made much progress. " Firmness " in the old sense is ruled out to-day as uneconomic—and we may still live to regret the fact. After " delight " many still strive—and most in vain. In this last pursuit, however, we might even now do well to take a lesson from the old cottages, which seem to grow in beauty as they age, or at least leave them in the peace of their maturity for the benefit of those who come after, caring for their fabrics solicitously, as we would care for the health of one whose long lifetime has been devoted to useful service.

GOTHICK CHAPTER-HOUSES FOR
LODGES, RENDLESHAM, SUFFOLK.

INDEX

(The numerals in italics denote the *figure numbers* of illustrations)